Revelation

Revelation
A Devotional Commentary

Edward B. Allen

Melbourne

Revelation: A Devotional Commentary
by Edward B. Allen
Copyright © 1999, 2016 by Edward B. Allen
All rights reserved.
Reprinted with revisions, 2017, 2020, 2021, 2026.

Published by Edward B. Allen
Melbourne, Florida
Email: edward.allen1949@gmail.com

ISBN: 978-0-9974147-3-8 (paperback)
978-0-9974147-4-5 (ebook *.epub)
978-0-9974147-5-2 (Kindle ebook *.mobi)

An earlier edition was published under the title, *Blessed is He who Reads: A Devotional Commentary on Revelation*, by Edward B. Allen © 1999.
Contact the publisher if you have questions regarding copying this book.
Unless otherwise noted, all scripture quotations are taken from the *Holman Christian Standard Bible*® (marked HCSB®), Copyright © 1999, 2000, 2002, 2003, 2009 by Holman Bible Publishers. Used by permission. HCSB® is a federally registered trademark of Holman Bible Publishers.
Scriptures quoted in this work are noted by the following abbreviations and follow usage guidelines of each publisher.

HCSB, Holman Christian Standard Bible, © 2009 Holman Bible Publishers
KJV, King James Version, pubic domain
NKJV, New King James Version, © 1983 Thomas Nelson, Inc.
NASB, New American Standard Bible, © 1995 Lockman Foundation
NIV, New International Version, © 2011 Biblica Inc.
AB, Amplified Bible, © 1965 Zondervan Publishing House

Cover design by Ken Raney (http://kenraney.com), based on a woodcut print by Albrecht Dürer.

To Angie

Contents

Illustrations	ix
Meditations	xi
Personal Studies	xiii
Preface	xv

1 Introduction — 1
    Alpha and Omega — 1
    Panorama — 4

2 Overcomers — 9
    Among the Lampstands — 11
    The Downtown Church — 14
    The Underground Church — 16
    The Permissive Church — 19
    Reverend Jezebel's Church — 21
    The Historic Church — 26
    The Obscure Church — 28
    The Suburban Church — 30
    Review — 32

3 Creation Groans — 35
    Holy, Holy, Holy — 37
    Horsemen and More — 43
    The Faithful — 49
    Bugle Calls — 53
        Incense — 55
        Catastrophes — 56
        My Witnesses — 63
        King of Kings — 69
    Review — 72

4 War — 77

- War in Heaven — 80
- Big Brother — 87
- A New Song — 91
- Three Weapons — 94
- Harvests — 98
- The Wrath of God — 101
  - The Choir — 101
  - Plagues — 103
  - Gathering for War — 107
  - Finished — 110
- Review — 111

5 Victory — 115

- The Fall of Civilization — 117
- The Defeat of Oppression — 128
- The End of Deception — 131
- The Last Enemy — 135
- The Liberation of Creation — 139
- The City of God — 141
- Down by the Riverside — 144
- Review — 145

6 Conclusion — 149

- Panorama — 149
- Come, Lord Jesus — 155

Appendix — 158

For Group Study — 159

- No-Homework Plan — 160
- In-Depth Plan — 161
- Overview Plan — 163
- Quick Overview Plan — 165

Index — 167

About the author — 179

Illustrations

2.1	The Overcomer (1:9–20)	10
3.1	A Throne in Heaven (4:1–11)	36
3.2	Four Horsemen (6:1–8)	42
3.3	The Fifth and Sixth Seals (6:9–17)	46
3.4	Sealing God's Faithful (7:1–17)	48
3.5	The Lamb of God (7:9-17)	50
3.6	Trumpets (8:1–12)	54
3.7	The Sixth Trumpet (9:13–19)	58
3.8	A Bitter-Sweet Book (10:1-11)	62
4.1	A Woman and the Dragon (12:1–17)	79
4.2	War in Heaven (12:7–12)	82
4.3	Beasts (12:18–14:20)	86
5.1	Babylon (17:1–19:21)	116
5.2	Satan Bound (20:1–10)	132

Meditations

A Promised Blessing	xvi
The Testimony of Martyrs	8
A Thief	25
The Creator	34
Bitter-Sweet	64
The Almighty	68
At the Mall	71
A Roaring Lion	76
Work that Lasts	93
For Who He Is	100
The Hail Storm	109
The Real Superhero	114
A Wedding Invitation	124
A New Housecoat	136
Reservations Suggested	148

Personal Studies

Prologue (1:1–8) 4
Among the Lampstands (1:9–20) 14
Ephesus (2:1–7) 16
Smyrna (2:8–11) 18
Pergamum (2:12–17) 20
The Church (John 15:9–17) 21
Thyatira (2:18–29) 24
Sardis (3:1–6) 27
Philadelphia (3:7–13) 30
Laodicea (3:14–22) 31
Review—Letters to Seven Churches (1:9–3:22) 33
The Throne of God (4:1–5:14) 41
The Lamb (Isaiah 52:14–53:12) 43
Six Seals (6:1–17) 49
Servants of God (7:1–17) 53
Incense (8:1–5) 56
Six Trumpets (8:6–9:21) 61
My Witnesses (10:1–11:13) 69
The Seventh Trumpet (11:14–19) 72
Review—A Scroll with Seven Seals (4:1–11:19) 75
The Dragon (12:1–17) 85
Beasts (12:18–13:18) 91
A New Song (14:1–5) 94
Three Angels (14:6–13) 97
Armor (Ephesians 6:10–20) 97
Reapings (14:14–20) 99
Songs (15:1–8) 103
Six Bowls (16:1–12) 107
Three Frogs (16:13–16) 108
The Seventh Bowl (16:17–21) 111
Review—Seven Signs (12:1–16:21) 113
The Fall of Babylon (17:1–19:10) 127
Beasts Defeated (19:11–21) 130
Washing Feet (John 13:1–16) 131
The Dragon Bound (20:1–10) 135

Judgment (20:11–15)	138
A New Heaven and New Earth (21:1–8)	140
The New Jerusalem (21:9–27)	143
The River of Life (22:1–5)	145
Review—Seven-Fold Victory (17:1–22:5)	146
Revelation as a Whole	155
Epilogue (22:6–21)	157

Preface

Many books on Revelation are on the shelves of Christian bookstores already. Why do we need another one? This book has a devotional emphasis, rather than the analytical approach of others. The goal of this book is to make Revelation interesting, understandable, and helpful to the Christian who has always avoided studying it. I want reading Revelation to stimulate your worship, to build your faith, and to equip you for Christian living.

The body of this book is commentary. This may not be a scholarly book, but I have benefited greatly over the years from Christian scholars. Sources are cited in the notes. The stories in this book are based on my personal recollections of actual people and events, unless otherwise indicated. Meditations are set apart, scattered through the book. Use them as occasions for personal application, prayer, and worship. Personal study questions at the end of each section stimulate you to think about the main ideas of Revelation. Most of the questions don't have a simple "right" answer. Keep looking for the main ideas. Plans for group study are in the appendix.

The *Holman Christian Standard Bible* (HCSB) is the basis for the study. Other translations are also satisfactory. There are a few quotes from other translations. Transliterated Hebrew and Greek words are in *italics*, mostly in notes. The notes refer to scripture references and word studies in commonly available references, such as *Vine's Expository Dictionary of Biblical Words* and Strong's *Exhaustive Concordance of the Bible* which includes Hebrew and Greek dictionaries. Strong's reference numbers for Hebrew and Greek words are used rather than full citations, for example, "(*Strong's* No. 2346)." Scripture references consist of book, chapter, verses, and version (if relevant), for example, "John 3:16 (KJV)." When Revelation is referenced, the book is omitted, for example, "1:3 (HCSB)." All scripture references are indexed.

The illustrations are woodcut prints by Albrecht Dürer (1498), courtesy of the Wetmore Print Collection at Connecticut College. I thank them for digitizing the prints and for permission to use them.

I thank the many friends who helped bring this book to maturity. Questions for discussion were first used at Christian Assembly, Vienna, Virginia. I thank Elizabeth Iatauro and Jim Croft for their thoughtful comments on an early manuscript. Finally, I am thankful for the steadfast support of my wife, Angie.

E.B.A

A Promised Blessing

Read 2 Peter 1:19–21.

Blessed is he who reads and those who hear the words of the prophecy, and heed the things which are written in it; for the time is near.[a]

Revelation 1:3 (NASB)

The letter from Toyota looked like official business. When I opened the envelope, I saw that they promised to reimburse me for repair of my car's transmission, but I had to follow the instructions to get any money.

The book of Revelation promises a blessing to whomever will read the instructions, hear what it has to say, and obey the instructions. I don't need to be a scholar to understand the Bible, because the Lord will help me. His Word shines on the path of my life. It is not just somebody's opinion. God's Word is reliable. If I will read the Bible, listen as it is read aloud, and do what it says, God will bless me.

PRAYER: Dear God, I want find out what the Bible teaches and obey your Word more consistently, especially the book of Revelation. Thank you for your promise. Amen.

---

[a]First beatitude of Revelation. There are seven verses in Revelation which say, "Blessed is he ..." or a similar phrase.

1

Introduction

The candlesticks, horsemen, whore, and beasts seemed strange. "God can't be this confusing," she said. "I'm sure thankful that salvation isn't this complicated." Angie had been a believer less than a year at the time. She thought a class might help. She listened intently when her adult Sunday school class studied the book of Revelation. "How did he get that out of this passage?" It just didn't make sense. She memorized a few well known scriptures from Revelation, but still didn't understand their context. Revelation became one of those books she just ignored.

This book was written for Angie, and those like her, who have never found the practical connection between Revelation and day-to-day Christian living. Many people miss God's message. Some start reading and immediately give up because of the symbolic language. A discouraged attitude is like ear plugs. Some try to see how it fits into a preconceived interpretation, "God's game plan for the universe." How can the Holy Spirit give fresh insights when we are only interested in proving our old ones? Some spend endless hours speculating on details, never appreciating the wholeness of God's message.

We don't have to wrestle alone with this book. God is on our side. He has promised to help us as we study Revelation.[1] Let us approach it prayerfully, openly, and expectantly.

Alpha and Omega

> Jesus Christ the same yesterday, and today, and for ever.
> Hebrews 13:8 (KJV)

Alpha is the first letter of the Greek alphabet, and omega is the last letter. Jesus spoke and the universe began,[2] and he will have the last word when history is finished. He is the Alpha and Omega. Revelation is a message to us from him.

---
[1] 1:3.
[2] Colossians 1:16.

Read this section's scripture passage.

Revelation 1:1–8 (HCSB)

---

1 The revelation of Jesus Christ that God gave Him to show His slaves what must quickly take place. He sent it and signified it through His angel to His slave John, 2 who testified to God's word and to the testimony about Jesus Christ, in all he saw. 3 The one who reads this is blessed, and those who hear the words of this prophecy and keep what is written in it are blessed, because the time is near!

4 John:
To the seven churches in Asia.

Grace and peace to you from the One who is, who was, and who is coming; from the seven spirits before His throne; 5 and from Jesus Christ, the faithful witness, the firstborn from the dead and the ruler of the kings of the earth.

To Him who loves us and has set us free from our sins by His blood, 6 and made us a kingdom, priests to His God and Father—the glory and dominion are His forever and ever. Amen.

> 7 Look! He is coming with the clouds,
> and every eye will see Him,
> including those who pierced Him.
> And all the families of the earth
> will mourn over Him.
> This is certain. Amen.

8 "I am the Alpha and the Omega," says the Lord God, "the One who is, who was, and who is coming, the Almighty."

The title of the book is "The revelation of Jesus Christ."[3] Jesus did not intend to confuse us; he wanted to reveal something to us. John carefully wrote everything down, so that we wouldn't miss anything. Therefore, we should approach this book expecting to understand it, and intending to put its teaching into practice. Applying the scriptures to our lives has practical benefits.

> All Scripture is inspired by God and is profitable for teaching, for rebuking, for correcting, for training in righteousness, so that the man of God may be complete, equipped for every good work.
> 2 Timothy 3:16–17 (HCSB)

When my uncle writes me a letter, he expects me to share it with my wife and the rest of the family. The book of Revelation was directly addressed to

---

[3] Revelation begins with the Greek word *apokalupsis* which means "an uncovering." W. E. Vine, *Vine's Expository Dictionary of Biblical Words* (Nashville: Thomas Nelson, 1985), s.v. *revelation*. This classic reference book defines key words of the Bible.

seven churches in the Roman province of Asia.[4] When God sent a letter to Christians in Asia, he expected them to share it with the rest of his family. The message is not limited to the addressees. It is also for us who have believed after them.

The letter begins with a blessing from God the Father, the Holy Spirit, and the Son. Certain characteristics of each one are emphasized. The Father is eternal. The Holy Spirit is before the throne of the Father. We can know the Father through Jesus. Jesus was the first one to rise from the dead never to die again, and he has all authority over the Earth.

Each point makes us meditate on who God is. This is the essence of worship. Having seen who God is, John lists things that Jesus has done for us: he loves us; he has freed us from sin; he has enabled us to serve God. This is the essence of praise. In ancient times, priests served God by offering sacrifices and performing other religious duties. We too, as believers, are a priesthood offering sacrifices of praise.

> But you are a chosen [nation], a royal priesthood, a holy nation, a people for His possession, so that you may proclaim the praises of the One who called you out of darkness into His marvelous light.
> 1 Peter 2:9 (HCSB)

Jesus promised that he will come back to Earth again, this time with power and glory. Those who do not believe, will mourn. We who do believe are eagerly waiting for that day. Even though Christians have many different interpretations of details about the second coming of Jesus, let us keep things simple by focusing on these points.

1. Jesus will personally return.

2. Believers will rise from the dead to eternal life.

3. Unbelievers will face eternal judgment.

4. Expect Him soon!

After Jesus ascended into the clouds, angels told the disciples that he will return in the same way.[5] Jesus himself said that he will come on the clouds with power and glory.[6] He will personally return. Paul explained that when Jesus returns those who have died in the Lord will be resurrected while believers who are alive at that time will be changed, and together we will be with Jesus forever thereafter.[7] This is eternal life. Throughout the Bible, it is clear that people will be judged for what they have done.[8] In particular, unbelievers will

---

[4]The Roman province of Asia was in the western part of modern Turkey.
[5]Acts 1:11.
[6]Matthew 24:30.
[7]1 Thessalonians 4:16–18 and 1 Corinthians 15:51–57.
[8]Hebrews 9:27.

face eternal judgment for their sin.[9] We don't know when Jesus is returning,[10] but we are confident that he will, and many will be surprised. We are eager to see him. God was here at the beginning, and he will be here at the end. He is the Alpha and Omega.

FOR PERSONAL STUDY
Prologue   (1:1–8)

1. What is the overall tone of these verses? What feelings emerge as you read?

2. List themes from the rest of the Bible which are suggested by the details of verses 4–8.

3. Which aspects of Jesus' character are emphasized?

4. Write a "thank you note" to God for the truth in these verses which is most special to you, like a birthday gift.

Panorama

> Blessed is he who reads and those who hear the words of the prophecy, and heed the things which are written in it; for the time is near.
>
> Revelation 1:3 (NASB)

This verse summarizes a well-known plan of Bible study, which we apply in this book to each passage.[11]

1. "he who reads ..."   What does it say?
2. "those who hear ..."   What does it mean?
3. "and [those who] heed ..." How does it apply to me?

Our study is based on the conviction that any ordinary Christian can read and understand the main ideas of Revelation, and find numerous personal applications for life today. Reading commentary alone is not a substitute for reading the Bible itself. Near the beginning of each section, you can read the passage in the *Holman Christian Standard Bible* (HCSB). Also read the passage from your own Bible, or even several translations together. You may want to

---

[9] 2 Peter 3:3–13.
[10] Matthew 24:44.
[11] James F. Nyquist and Jack Kuhatschek, *Leading Bible Discussions* (Downers Grove, IL: InterVarsity Press, 1985). This approach is used by many other Bible study books also. Nyquist and Kuhatschek explain how to lead inductive Bible studies, i.e., a discussion in a small group. This may be useful if you follow one of the group study plans in the appendix below. This book is a classic, but is not about Revelation.

Panorama

compare a paraphrase to a more literal translation. By comparing several translations, one can avoid overemphasis on individual words. Understanding the words of Revelation is not difficult.

An outline is an essential tool for studying Revelation. The following is our outline.

Prologue		1:1–8
I. Letters to Seven Churches		
Introduction	Among the Lampstands	1:9–20
1. Ephesus		2:1–7
2. Smyrna		2:8–11
3. Pergamum		2:12–17
4. Thyatira		2:18–29
5. Sardis		3:1–6
6. Philadelphia		3:7–13
7. Laodicea		3:14–22
II. A Scroll with Seven Seals		
Introduction	The Throne of God	4:1–5:14
1st Seal	A White Horse	6:1–2
2nd Seal	A Red Horse	6:3–4
3rd Seal	A Black Horse	6:5–6
4th Seal	A Pale Horse	6:7–8
5th Seal	Martyrs	6:9–11
6th Seal	Upheaval	6:12–17
Interlude	Servants of God	7:1–17
7th Seal	Seven Trumpets	
Introduction	Incense	8:1–5
1st Trumpet	Trees	8:6–7
2nd Trumpet	Sea	8:8–9
3rd Trumpet	Rivers and Springs	8:10–11
4th Trumpet	Sun, Moon, Stars	8:12
5th Trumpet	Torment	8:13–9:11
6th Trumpet	Fire, Smoke, Sulfur	9:12–21
Interlude	My Witnesses	10:1–11:13
7th Trumpet	Christ Reigns	11:14–19
III. Seven Signs		
1. The Dragon		12:1–17

2. Beasts		12:18–13:18
3. A New Song		14:1–5
4. 1st Angel	The Gospel	14:6–7
5. 2nd Angel	Babylon's Doom	14:8
6. 3rd Angel	Marked	14:9–13
Interlude	Reapings	14:14–20
7. Seven Bowls		
Introduction	Songs	15:1–8
1st Bowl	Sores	16:1–2
2nd Bowl	Sea	16:3
3rd Bowl	Rivers and Springs	16:4–7
4th Bowl	Sun	16:8–9
5th Bowl	Darkness	16:10–11
6th Bowl	The Euphrates	16:12
Interlude	Three frogs	16:13–16
7th Bowl	Finished	16:17–21
IV. Seven-Fold Victory		
1. The Fall of Babylon		17:1–19:10
2. Beasts Defeated		19:11–21
3. The Dragon Bound		20:1–10
4. Judgment		20:11–15
5. A New Heaven and New Earth		21:1–8
6. The New Jerusalem		21:9–27
7. The River of Life		22:1–5
Epilogue		22:6–21

This outline is based on literary structure, without assuming any particular interpretation. The outline was the seed for later interpretation. When one compares commentators' outlines of Revelation, it is clear why their interpretations differ so much.

There are many interpretations of Revelation. You or your pastor might prefer a different interpretation than mine. A difference in interpretation should never disrupt our fellowship in the Lord. Love for one another is more important than opinions.[12] My interpretation is my opinion. I don't mind if you disagree with my opinions.

Our goal is to find interpretations that capture the main ideas and the impact of the passages. A valid interpretation cannot contradict biblical teaching as a whole. The simple meaning of the original Greek and Hebrew Scriptures

---

[12] 1 Corinthians 13:2.

should be sufficient, without resorting to deciphering code words. God's Word is for all God's people. So a sound interpretation should be general enough to be meaningful across the centuries and across cultures. God's Word is profitable, applicable to the Christian life. An interpretation should reflect these qualities of God's Word.

Revelation is not direct teaching. It describes John's visions and is highly symbolic, so interpreting all the details is difficult and error-prone. Consequently, controversies over interpretations are all too common, disrupting love for one another. Instead of basing doctrines of the faith on symbols in Revelation, we let Revelation illuminate doctrines and principles that are clearly presented in other scriptures. This is the reason that the above doctrinal points about the second coming of Jesus are based on scriptures other than Revelation.

In contrast to many other commentators, we approach Revelation as a panorama, a large tapestry, rather than as a predictive chronology of the second coming of Jesus. A panorama is relevant to Christians in all eras.

Even though an interpretation may be quite general, an application is often very specific to life today. Although many of the visions in Revelation seem global in scope, we will apply the lessons to our local situations. Some of the details may not be fulfilled in our local situations, but we can apply the main idea anyway. These are the major themes which we will apply to our lives through this study.

1. The church must overcome.

2. The world must repent.

3. The devil is angry.

4. Jesus wins.

The Lord wants each local group of Christians to overcome their spiritual challenges. He is there to help. The Lord wants all people to repent from sin and receive his life.[13] Satan is angry, and so he wants to destroy all that God loves, but we know that Jesus who has risen from the dead will be victorious in the end.

Most of the examples in this book are in the context of American culture, because that is where I live. Look for the parallels in your own life. Applying Revelation to our lives will be more than an intellectual exercise. It will require our practical obedience to what God says to us.

---

[13] 2 Peter 3:9.

The Testimony of Martyrs

Read Luke 21:12–19.

> When He opened the fifth seal, I saw under the altar the people slaughtered because of God's word and the testimony they had.
>
> Revelation 6:9 (HCSB)

In February 2015, the Islamic State published a video showing the beheading of twenty-one Christians in Libya.[a] They were migrant workers from Egypt and one from Chad. The Islamic State had kidnapped the workers less than two months before. They were executed simply because their captors hated Christians.

The man from Chad was originally a non-Christian, but had converted when he saw the faith of the others. He had the opportunity to deny Christ and save his life, but he remained faithful.

The twenty-one who were killed will surely receive a martyr's reward from the hand of Jesus.

PRAYER: Dear God, protect, uphold and strengthen those who are being persecuted, like the brothers and sisters in Libya. Make them effective witnesses for you. Amen.

---

[a] "2015 kidnapping and beheading of Copts in Libya," *Wikipedia*. Available at http://en.wikipedia.org.

2

Overcomers

> In the world you will have tribulation; but be of good cheer, I have overcome the world.
>
> John 16:33 (NKJV)

The apostle Paul knew hardships first hand. Shortly after his conversion, he had to sneak out of Damascus to escape assassination. In Lystra, an angry mob thought they had killed him. On his way to Rome, his ship was destroyed in a storm. Through it all, he felt like a conqueror, because he knew Jesus loved him.[1] We too can overcome opposition and obstacles, because God's love is always there, and Jesus has already overcome the world.

> For I am persuaded that not even death or life, angels or rulers, things present or things to come, hostile powers, height or depth, or any other created thing will have the power to separate us from the love of God that is in Christ Jesus our Lord!
>
> Romans 8:38–39 (HCSB)

In the following sections, we study the remainder of chapter 1 of Revelation as well as chapters 2 and 3 to see what Jesus had to say to seven churches. We can then apply that message to our own Christian circles. As shown in the following outline, chapter 1 has a detailed description of Jesus standing among seven lampstands. Chapters 2 and 3 are letters from Jesus to seven churches. Each church had different strengths and problems, but each letter makes a promise "to him who overcomes" (NASB).[2]

I. Letters to Seven Churches

    Introduction   Among the Lampstands   1:9–20

---

[1] Acts 9:22–25, Acts 14:19–20, Acts 27:41–44, and Romans 8:35–37.
[2] 2:7, 2:11, 2:17, 2:26–28, 3:5, 3:12, and 3:21.

Illustration 2.1: The Overcomer (1:9–20)

1. Ephesus	2:1–7
2. Smyrna	2:8–11
3. Pergamum	2:12–17
4. Thyatira	2:18–29
5. Sardis	3:1–6
6. Philadelphia	3:7–13
7. Laodicea	3:14–22

Among the Lampstands

He was waiting in the airport for the next flight like everyone else, but much of his career was obvious to anyone who could interpret his symbols. His hat indicated his country. His green coat and black shoes hinted who his employer was. The colorful patch on his upper sleeve belonged to his department. Stripes on his sleeve said what his salary range was. Bars on his forearm counted years of service. The pins decorating his left chest pocket told of his courage and determination. His name was over his right chest pocket. The symbols spoke loud and plain to those who knew their meaning. He was in the United States Army.

The first chapter's description of Jesus seems like a jumble of symbols. What do they all mean? "I'm not used to figuring out symbols," one might protest. We interpret symbols in daily life more than we realize. Read this section's Scripture passage.

Revelation 1:9–20 (HCSB)

---

9 I, John, your brother and partner in the tribulation, kingdom, and endurance that are in Jesus, was on the island called Patmos because of God's word and the testimony about Jesus. 10 I was in the Spirit on the Lord's day, and I heard a loud voice behind me like a trumpet 11 saying, "Write on a scroll what you see and send it to the seven churches: Ephesus, Smyrna, Pergamum, Thyatira, Sardis, Philadelphia, and Laodicea."

12 I turned to see whose voice it was that spoke to me. When I turned I saw seven gold lampstands, 13 and among the lampstands was One like the Son of Man, dressed in a long robe and with a gold sash wrapped around His chest. 14 His head and hair were white like wool—white as snow—and His eyes like a fiery flame. 15 His feet were like fine bronze as it is fired in a furnace, and His voice like the sound of cascading waters. 16 He had seven stars in His right hand; a sharp double-edged sword came from His mouth, and His face was shining like the sun at midday.

17 When I saw Him, I fell at His feet like a dead man. He laid His right hand on me and said, "Don't be afraid! I am the First and the Last, 18 and the Living One. I was dead, but look—I am alive forever and ever, and I hold the keys of death and Hades. 19 Therefore write what you have seen, what is, and what will take place after this. 20 The secret of the seven stars you saw in My right hand and of the seven gold lampstands is this: The seven stars are the angels of the seven churches, and the seven lampstands are the seven churches.

Interpreting Revelation is not hard, because God has provided help. When reading Revelation, some symbols are directly explained in the passage. Other symbols remind us of other scriptures where the meaning of a similar symbol is clear. John expected us to be familiar with the Bible, especially the Old Testament, the Jewish scriptures. Sometimes common things of everyday life at the time Revelation was written in the first century AD give insight, too. Understanding the major ideas of Revelation is something an ordinary person can do. You do not need to be a theology expert.

John was isolated on the island of Patmos for the sake of the gospel. He could identify with the persecution faced by those he was writing to. The word translated *tribulation* in 1:9 (KJV) primarily means pressure.[3] This word appears numerous times in the New Testament referring to various kinds of suffering and persecution. In some passages, it is translated affliction. We should be careful not to make such a common word into a specialized theological concept. At the time Revelation was written, Christians were severely persecuted by the Roman authorities and by the Jewish community. John himself was in exile on Patmos. We can draw parallels between pressures on Christians then and today, and then apply what we learn to pressures in our own lives.

As John's vision began, he was told to write to the local church in seven specific cities on the mainland in the nearby Roman province of Asia: Ephesus, Smyrna, Pergamum, Thyatira, Sardis, Philadelphia, and Laodicea. He then saw Jesus, the risen Christ. The description of Jesus that follows introduces letters to the seven churches from Jesus. Although written over nineteen hundred years ago, the letters to the seven churches speak to the church today. They apply not only to the church at the corner, but also to Sunday school classes, youth groups, campus ministries, home Bible studies, parachurch organizations, and so on. The same strengths and problems are there, and Jesus still offers the same promises.

The description of Jesus reminds us of his appearance during the transfiguration.[4] This association reinforces what we saw earlier in chapter 1; Jesus, the

---

[3]Vine, *s.v. affliction* and *s.v. tribulation*. The Greek word *thlipsis* (*Strong's* No. 2346). J. Strong, *Exhaustive Concordance of the Bible* (1894). This classic reference book includes Hebrew and Greek dictionaries. Strong's reference numbers for words are often used by other reference books, including the notes in this book.

[4]Matthew 17:1–2.

Son of God, is eternal.[5] His golden sash, his flaming eyes, his feet of bronze, and his voice of rushing waters also remind us of Daniel's vision where he is a messenger, sent to reveal a vision.[6] Similarly, Jesus is a messenger with a vision for the church. The sword[7] from his mouth with two sharp edges, is a reference to the word of God.

> For the word of God is living and effective and sharper than any double-edged sword, penetrating as far as the separation of soul and spirit, joints and marrow. It is able to judge the ideas and thoughts of the heart.
>
> Hebrews 4:12 (HCSB)

The Bible is the written expression of God's thoughts,[8] and reading it, we encounter this living and active sword. In Ephesians, we are told to put on the armor of God, including a sword.

> Take the helmet of salvation, and the sword of the Spirit, which is God's word.
>
> Ephesians 6:17 (HCSB)

Because words are spoken,[9] it is natural for the sword to come out of his mouth. This "word of God" is what the Holy Spirit personally tells us. Frequently, the word of God is a personal application of the Bible, the Word of God.

This shining messenger identified himself as the risen Christ, the one who has conquered death. Jesus himself explained the seven stars and the seven lampstands of the vision. The seven stars in his hand were angels assigned to the seven churches. The seven lampstands signified the seven churches themselves. Jesus was standing in the middle of them.

Jesus is present at every worship service, Sunday school class, social function, and committee meeting. The church is not just an organization to perpetuate his memory. It is a body of people that he lives among.

> For where two or three are gathered together in My name, I am there among them.
>
> Matthew 18:20 (HCSB)

---

[5] 1:8.

[6] Daniel 10:5–6.

[7] The Greek word *rhomphaia* (*Strong's* No. 4501) in 1:16 means a long saber. The Greek word *machaira* (*Strong's* No. 3162), meaning a knife or a personal weapon, is much more common throughout the New Testament, including both Ephesians 6:17 and Hebrews 4:12. The word from Jesus' mouth pierces soul and spirit as deep as a saber, and *rhema* and *logos* are personal weapons of spiritual warfare.

[8] The Greek word *logos* (*Strong's* No. 3056) in Hebrews 4:12 is defined as the expression of a thought.

[9] 1:16. The Greek word *rhema* (*Strong's* No. 4487) in Ephesians 6:17 is defined as something spoken.

FOR PERSONAL STUDY
Among the Lampstands (1:9–20)

1. Draw a large simple picture of a man. Write each literal item in verses 12–16 on the picture in its proper place.

2. Draw another large picture of a man. Write the personal qualities you associate with each item on the first picture, in its proper place. (Note that verse 20 helps interpret some items.)

3. Which aspects of Jesus' character are repeated from verses 4–8?

4. How do symbols affect you intellectually and emotionally, compared to a straight description of abstract character qualities?

The Downtown Church

I was a first-time visitor. I knew the church had a good reputation. When I saw the crowded sanctuary, I thought, "They must be friendly here," but no one greeted me. There was a map in the foyer showing the missionaries they support. I recognized some well known ministries. I thought, "They are reaching the world for God." The bulletin listed something going on every night. I thought, "These folks are dedicated." They announced there would be a famous guest preacher next Sunday. I could tell they didn't let just anybody fill the pulpit. After the benediction, the church was empty in a few minutes, and this visitor felt alone. They were busy for God, but there was no time left for loving God and neighbor.[10]

Jesus had a message for the downtown church. Read the letter to Ephesus.

Revelation 2:1–7 (HCSB)

> 1 "Write to the angel of the church in Ephesus:
> "The One who holds the seven stars in His right hand and who walks among the seven gold lampstands says: 2 I know your works, your labor, and your endurance, and that you cannot tolerate evil. You have tested those who call themselves apostles and are not, and you have found them to be liars. 3 You also possess endurance and have tolerated many things because of My name and have not grown weary. 4 But I have this against you: You have abandoned the love you had at first. 5 Remember then how far you have fallen; repent, and do the works you did at first. Otherwise, I will come to you and remove your lampstand from its place—unless you repent. 6 Yet you do have this: You hate the practices of the Nicolaitans, which I also hate.

---
[10] Matthew 22:36–40.

> 7 "Anyone who has an ear should listen to what the Spirit says to the churches. I will give the victor the right to eat from the tree of life, which is in God's paradise.

Above all, Jesus wants to have an intimate love-relationship with us, and from that will flow love for others and service for him. You can't trick Jesus. He has the church in his hand, and he walks among the churches. He knows all about our accomplishments, and he knows our hidden weaknesses.

The church in Ephesus was started by Paul and had grown over the years. By the time John wrote Revelation, it had become one of the world's great churches. It had many effective programs. It had a tradition of great Bible teachers. They always investigated visiting preachers, so that the flock of God would not be led astray. It was a strong church. Its leaders had international reputations. It was the church where everybody who wanted to be respectable was a member.

However, Jesus knew there was a problem. They had left their "first love" (KJV). We, too, should be careful to keep our love for Jesus fresh. An intimate relationship with him is more important than effective programs, great Bible studies, and an international reputation. We can cultivate our love for Jesus in personal prayer and meditation, in corporate worship, and in love for one another.

Loving someone requires time together. I used to try to spend time in prayer and Bible reading just before going to bed, but I kept falling asleep. Then I tried to do it in the morning, but it was hard to get out of bed. I discovered that the key to personal time with Jesus was the discipline of going to bed early to get adequate rest. My love for Jesus has grown deeper as we have spent that intimate time together in prayer and Bible reading.

Corporate worship is how a church congregation expresses love for Jesus. It is so refreshing when the worship service doesn't seem rushed, when there is time to focus on the Lord while singing and praying together, and when he is more important than plans to eat at the restaurant after the service. Going beyond a worship service, love for Jesus naturally expresses itself in love for other believers.

> By this all people will know that you are My disciples, if you have love for one another.
>
> John 13:35 (HCSB)

Love for one another does not happen just on Sunday. It is expressed throughout the week, in ordinary situations, in practical living. This is the love that isn't too busy to listen, that isn't too busy to help, that isn't too busy to sacrifice personal convenience for a fellow believer.

Even though Ephesus had lost its first love, Jesus commended them for not following the Nicolaitans. Although scholars do not agree over historical details about the Nicolaitans in the time of John, we do know that they taught false doctrine.[11] We can apply the warning about the Nicolaitans to any group today that teaches a subversive doctrine.

The promise to overcomers at Ephesus is the right to eat of the tree of life. The tree of life was in the Garden of Eden.[12] Because of sin, Adam and Eve were forced to leave God's paradise and were prevented from eating from the tree of life.[13] Even though mankind lost the privilege of eternal life, that is not the end of the story. Those who have that first love for Jesus will be welcomed into the God's garden to eat from the tree of life.

When my wife and I became engaged, life suddenly became very busy. Rather than get swallowed up by all the things we had to do and let our first love get cold, we set aside one night each week for a date. We didn't necessarily go anyplace, but we did spend the time together sharing with each other. Looking back, that time was vital to starting a healthy marriage. A regular date has been a good idea since the wedding, too. Time with Jesus is just as important.

FOR PERSONAL STUDY
Ephesus   (2:1–7)

1. Characterize Ephesus' virtues in a short phrase.

2. What was their problem?

3. Describe a hypothetical modern church like Ephesus.

4. What aspects of Jesus' character are emphasized in verse 1? How are they related to the situation at Ephesus?

5. What was the overall message to Ephesus?

6. Are you a member of a Christian group that is like Ephesus? How is it similar? How is it different?

The Underground Church

In ancient Rome, the persecuted church met secretly in the tunnels of the cemetery, the catacombs. They were the original underground church. Today, Christians still face persecution in many parts of the world.

When my wife and I visited China in 1998, we met a student who insisted that we attend an underground church meeting. It seemed risky, but we took a taxi with him to an industrial block where a factory and apartments for the workers were all within a walled city block. We walked past the armed guard and went up the stairs to an apartment which soon filled with about twenty believers.

---

[11] 2:6 and 2:15.
[12] Genesis 2:8–9.
[13] Genesis 3:22–24.

The Underground Church

Registered churches in China are monitored by the Communist Party. Unregistered Christian groups must meet secretly. The severity of persecution of Christians in China varies from place to place and from time to time according to the attitudes of the authorities. This group had the freedom to sing Christian songs in the apartment, but had to go to a remote countryside location for baptisms. A traditional church service might have resulted in leaders going to jail. So, their Easter worship service consisted of prayer-walking among the tourists on the ancient city wall, interceding for their city.

Jesus had a message for the underground church. Read the letter to Smyrna.

Revelation 2:8–11 (HCSB)

---

8 "Write to the angel of the church in Smyrna:

"The First and the Last, the One who was dead and came to life, says: 9 I know your affliction and poverty, yet you are rich. I know the slander of those who say they are Jews and are not, but are a synagogue of Satan. 10 Don't be afraid of what you are about to suffer. Look, the Devil is about to throw some of you into prison to test you, and you will have affliction for 10 days. Be faithful until death, and I will give you the crown of life.

11 "Anyone who has an ear should listen to what the Spirit says to the churches. The victor will never be harmed by the second death.

Jesus is the second person of the Trinity. He is eternal. He is the author and completer of our faith.[14] He knew what death was like; he died on the cross. He also knew what victory is like; he rose on the third day.

Jesus knew what life in Smyrna was like. Life for Christians was tough. They were poor, slandered, jailed, and sometimes killed for the name of Jesus. They probably had to meet secretly. When we face adversity, it is tempting to fall into self pity, thinking, "No one understands what I'm going through." However, in reality, Jesus understands our situation and how we feel better than anyone. Sometimes the joy of the Christian life is portrayed as though problems never happen. If anything, being a believer brings trials with it.

> Dear friends, don't be surprised when the fiery ordeal comes among you to test you as if something unusual were happening to you. Instead, rejoice as you share in the sufferings of the Messiah, so that you may also rejoice with great joy at the revelation of His glory. If you are ridiculed for the name of Christ, you are blessed, because the Spirit of glory and of God rests on you. None of you, however, should suffer as a murderer, a thief, an evildoer, or a meddler. But if anyone suffers as a "Christian," he should not be ashamed but should glorify God in having that name.
>
> 1 Peter 4:12–16 (HCSB)

---

[14] Hebrews 12:2 (KJV).

In this passage, Peter explains that persecution is a natural result of following Jesus. Smyrna was not an unusual church. In fact, we should expect to be like them—persecuted and glad to represent Jesus in this world.

Jesus promised that Smyrna's persecution was only a short test. The time period of ten days reminds us of Daniel's test.

> "Please test your servants for 10 days. Let us be given vegetables to eat and water to drink. Then examine our appearance and the appearance of the young men who are eating the king's food, and deal with your servants based on what you see." He agreed with them about this and tested them for 10 days.
>
> Daniel 1:12–14 (HCSB)

Daniel and his friends were away from home at an elite school. Rather than blend in with the crowd, they stood up for following the Lord. They were allowed ten days to prove that obeying God's dietary laws was as good as eating from the King's table. It seemed like a pretty short test period. At the end of the test period, they were better than the crowd.

The purpose of a test is to prove that following Jesus is better than following the crowd. Smyrna was found faithful. Like their ten days, the test of our faith won't last forever. At the end of Smyrna's test period, they will receive a crown of life, rather than the second death. The second death is defined later in Revelation as a lake of fire,[15] which was prepared for Satan, his agents of oppression, and even death itself. Those who side with Satan, go there with him. The lake of fire is the traditional fiery picture of "damnation in hell."

That little band of Chinese Christians was standing faithful. Even if direct persecution arises in their city, natural death, the first death, will not be intimidating. It is temporary, compared to eternal suffering in the lake of fire, the second death.

FOR PERSONAL STUDY
Smyrna   (2:8–11)

1. What was it like in Smyrna for the Christians?

2. How is the description of Jesus in verse 8 related to their situation?

3. Summarize Jesus' message to Smyrna in slang terms.

4. Are you a member of a Christian group that is like Smyrna? How is it similar? How is it different?

---

[15] 20:14.

The Permissive Church

A wave of ecumenical enthusiasm had swept the campus. Denominational barriers had fallen among the Protestants and all backgrounds participated in common campus worship services. By the time I arrived on campus as a freshman, there was such tolerance for opinions that Bible study was not on the schedule. Jesus was rarely mentioned. Worship was advertised as a "celebration of life" and preaching consisted of calls to political action. Something had been lost.

Jesus had a message for the permissive church. Read the letter to Pergamum.

Revelation 2:12–17 (HCSB)

---

12 "Write to the angel of the church in Pergamum:

"The One who has the sharp, double-edged sword says: 13 I know where you live—where Satan's throne is! And you are holding on to My name and did not deny your faith in Me, even in the days of Antipas, My faithful witness who was killed among you, where Satan lives. 14 But I have a few things against you. You have some there who hold to the teaching of Balaam, who taught Balak to place a stumbling block in front of the Israelites: to eat meat sacrificed to idols and to commit sexual immorality. 15 In the same way, you also have those who hold to the teaching of the Nicolaitans. 16 Therefore repent! Otherwise, I will come to you quickly and fight against them with the sword of My mouth.

17 "Anyone who has an ear should listen to what the Spirit says to the churches. I will give the victor some of the hidden manna. I will also give him a white stone, and on the stone a new name is inscribed that no one knows except the one who receives it.

When John saw Jesus, he had a sharp double-edged sword coming out of his mouth, which, we saw, represents the word of God.

Pergamum was in a rough neighborhood. Satan lived there. It was violent. Brother Antipas had been killed for the gospel. Even so, they remained true to the Lord.

However, there were a few problems. Rather than reject the Nicolaitans, as Ephesus had done, Pergamum tolerated that group. There were some in the church who taught false doctrine, like Balaam in the Old Testament.[16] Balaam is famous among Bible characters because a donkey warned him. He was a prophet who was motivated by greed, and Balak from Moab was willing to pay handsomely if Balaam would pronounce a curse on Israel.

> They have eyes full of adultery and are always looking for sin. They seduce unstable people and have hearts trained in greed. Children

---

[16] Numbers 22:1–25:5.

> under a curse! They have gone astray by abandoning the straight path and have followed the path of Balaam, the son of Bosor, who loved the wages of unrighteousness but received a rebuke for his transgression: A donkey that could not talk spoke with a human voice and restrained the prophet's irrationality.
>
> 2 Peter 2:14–16 (HCSB)

Even though he did not prophesy against Israel with his words, he did teach Balak how to seduce Israel into immorality and idolatry. The teachers in Pergamum were leading the people away from the Lord into idolatry and immorality. If they were like Balaam, their motive was greed.

Christians who tolerate all kinds of teaching are like Pergamum. It is a mistake to be so broad-minded that one excuses violations of the clear teaching of the Bible. When a permissive attitude reigns, it becomes normal to worship things rather than the Lord, and to live an immoral lifestyle.

Jesus warned them to repent. Otherwise, the word of God will deal with them. To those who overcome, Jesus will give true nourishment, "hidden manna" representing the word of God.

> He humbled you by letting you go hungry; then He gave you manna to eat, which you and your fathers had not known, so that you might learn that man does not live on bread alone but on every word that comes from the mouth of the Lord.
>
> Deuteronomy 8:3 (HCSB)

After the Israelites left Egypt with Moses, God fed them in the desert with manna, a small white substance that looked like frost,[17] which they baked into bread. Jesus is the source of the true manna that nourishes the soul. He is the bread of life. He is the answer to false teaching.

> "I am the bread of life," Jesus told them. "No one who comes to Me will ever be hungry, and no one who believes in Me will ever be thirsty again."
>
> John 6:35 (HCSB)

FOR PERSONAL STUDY
Pergamum   (2:12–17)

1. Describe some neighborhoods today where a church "dwells where Satan's seat is"?

2. What was the general problem at Pergamum?

3. Review Numbers 22:1–25:5. How does the story of Balaam help us understand Pergamum's problem?

---

[17] Exodus 16:14–15.

4. What does the two-edged sword represent? How does the two-edged sword relate to their problem?

5. What did Jesus want Pergamum to do?

6. Are you a member of a Christian group that is like Pergamum? How is it similar? How is it different?

FOR PERSONAL STUDY
The Church   (John 15:9–17)

Read John 15:9–17.

1. Read John 13:35. When we see a group of people gathered in a building with a steeple, how do we know whether they are a "church"?

2. List the characteristics of God's love:

   - Where is it from?
   - How big is it?
   - What fruit does it produce?

3. Describe the kind of relationships Christians are commanded to have with each other.

4. Why do you think Jesus gave this commandment?

5. List some practical actions and attitudes that cultivate love for one another.

Reverend Jezebel's Church

On November 18, 1978, 909 people died in a mass suicide and murder in Jonestown, Guyana, South America.[18] They were members of the People's Temple, a religious group in California led by Reverend Jim Jones, who also committed suicide. The People's Temple teaching centered on "Dad," a title Jones took for himself. He demanded total allegiance. Jones was personally involved in political corruption, adultery, homosexuality, and drug addiction. An investigation of oppressive conditions at the Guyana community resulted in the murder of a Congressman and others. As law enforcement closed in, Jones ordered the ritualistic mass suicide.

Jesus had a message for Reverend Jezebel's church. Read the letter to Thyatira.

---

[18] Richard C. Schroeder, "Jonestown," *The Encyclopedia Americana*, International Edition, vol. 16 (Danbury, Connecticut: Grolier, 1987), *s.v. Jonestown*.

Revelation 2:18–29 (HCSB)

18 "Write to the angel of the church in Thyatira:

"The Son of God, the One whose eyes are like a fiery flame and whose feet are like fine bronze, says: 19 I know your works—your love, faithfulness, service, and endurance. Your last works are greater than the first. 20 But I have this against you: You tolerate the woman Jezebel, who calls herself a prophetess and teaches and deceives My slaves to commit sexual immorality and to eat meat sacrificed to idols. 21 I gave her time to repent, but she does not want to repent of her sexual immorality. 22 Look! I will throw her into a sickbed and those who commit adultery with her into great tribulation, unless they repent of her practices. 23 I will kill her children with the plague. Then all the churches will know that I am the One who examines minds and hearts, and I will give to each of you according to your works. 24 I say to the rest of you in Thyatira, who do not hold this teaching, who haven't known the deep things of Satan—as they say—I do not put any other burden on you. 25 But hold on to what you have until I come. 26 The one who is victorious and keeps My works to the end: I will give him authority over the nations—

27 and he will shepherd them with an iron scepter;
he will shatter them like pottery—

just as I have received this from My Father. 28 I will also give him the morning star.

29 "Anyone who has an ear should listen to what the Spirit says to the churches.

The eyes of Jesus can see the true situation. His feet can trample sin and corruption. He is the Son of God, vested with all authority by the Father. He is the one who spoke to Thyatira.

He commended them for their accomplishments and spiritual fruit of love, faith, and patience. They were serving the Lord more and more. This was a commendation any church would be thrilled to receive. However, there was a problem.

The church tolerated a corrupt leader, a so-called prophetess, who was like Jezebel in the Old Testament. Jezebel was the wife of Ahab, king of the northern kingdom of Israel.[19] Jezebel was from the Canaanite city of Sidon. Ahab and Jezebel fostered a resurgence of Canaanite idolatry in Israel more than any of the kings before him.

Paul warns us to be on guard against such people. They sound good, but their motives are selfish, and their fruit is strife.

---

[19] 1 Kings 16:29–33.

> Now I urge you, brothers, to watch out for those who cause dissensions and obstacles contrary to the doctrine you have learned. Avoid them, for such people do not serve our Lord Christ but their own appetites. They deceive the hearts of the unsuspecting with smooth talk and flattering words.
>
> Romans 16:17–18 (HCSB)

Thyatira's Jezebel needed to be disciplined, not only for her own sake, but also because she was misleading others into sinful lifestyles. The New Testament clearly teaches that the church as a whole is to discipline those who fall into sin. Jesus gave us step by step instructions.

> If your brother sins against you, go and rebuke him in private. If he listens to you, you have won your brother. But if he won't listen, take one or two more with you, so that by the testimony of two or three witnesses every fact may be established. If he pays no attention to them, tell the church. But if he doesn't pay attention even to the church, let him be like an unbeliever and a tax collector to you.
>
> Matthew 18:15–17 (HCSB)

This procedure can be applied to a male or female Jezebel today. Correction in a Biblical manner, with a proper attitude, and by proper authority in the church is sometimes needed.

God gave the Jezebel in Thyatira and her followers the opportunity to repent, and he will hold them accountable for their actions. Hearts and minds are not hidden from his penetrating gaze. Sin is crushed under his bronze feet.

Jesus told a parable about weeds growing among grain. Later, he explained the parable to his disciples. The devil secretly puts his people among the believers. They may grow up together, but eventually, Jesus will separate them.

> The field is the world; and the good seed—these are the sons of the kingdom. The weeds are the sons of the evil one, and the enemy who sowed them is the Devil. The harvest is the end of the age, and the harvesters are angels. Therefore, just as the weeds are gathered and burned in the fire, so it will be at the end of the age. The Son of Man will send out His angels, and they will gather from His kingdom everything that causes sin and those guilty of lawlessness. They will throw them into the blazing furnace where there will be weeping and gnashing of teeth. Then the righteous will shine like the sun in their Father's kingdom. Anyone who has ears should listen!
>
> Matthew 13:38–43 (HCSB)

Jezebel was a weed in the field of Thyatira. God had allowed her to be among his people temporarily.

Because Thyatira's church was already under the control of Jezebel, Jesus did not impose harsh requirements on those who had remained faithful there.

He told them, "Only hold on to what you have until I come."[20] There are times when a corrupt leader so dominates a church that the procedure for Biblical correction does not produce repentance. In such cases, Jesus wants each church member simply to be faithful.

The authorities in the church at Thyatira may have been corrupt, but Jesus promised proper authority.

> I will declare the Lord's decree: He said to Me, "You are My Son; today I have become Your Father. Ask of Me, and I will make the nations Your inheritance and the ends of the earth Your possession. You will break them with a rod of iron; You will shatter them like pottery."
>
> Psalms 2:7–9 (HCSB)

This psalm prophesied that the Messiah will have complete authority over the nations, represented by the iron scepter. Jesus promised to delegate that authority to the overcomers in Thyatira.

Jesus also promised them the "morning star." This is a reference to the Messiah himself, who will completely defeat idolatry.[21]

FOR PERSONAL STUDY
Thyatira (2:18–29)

1. Compare this passage in the King James Version and a modern translation. List phrases which are different. Are any of the differences surprising?

2. Describe the situation at Thyatira.

3. What are the differences between the problems of Pergamum and Thyatira?

4. What was the church at Thyatira told to do concerning Jezebel?

5. What Christian virtue is being emphasized for the believers in Thyatira?

6. What is the main idea of Jesus' message to Thyatira?

7. Do you know a church leader whose corruption is as serious as Jezebel's in Thyatira?

---

[20] 2:25 (NIV).
[21] Numbers 24:17.

A Thief

Read Luke 12:35–40.

Behold, I am coming like a thief. Blessed is the one who stays awake and keeps his garments.[a]

Revelation 16:15 (NASB)

"What's going on? I thought there were three pieces of bait here." My Dad and I were fishing in the Florida surf using pieces of raw fish for bait. The old board that served as a cutting block was right behind me. No one could have taken the extra bait without my noticing, and besides, the beach was deserted.

Then my Dad laughed. He saw the thief a few feet away. Over by the sand dune, a blue heron was standing like a statue. That thief had made his move when I wasn't looking.

Jesus said that his coming will be unexpected, just like a thief. No one knows when he is coming, but we can be prepared. I don't want to be caught with an apathetic attitude. I don't want him to find me with a grudge in my heart. So, whenever a little sin creeps into my life, I immediately ask God for forgiveness and cleansing.

The beach may look deserted, but the Lord is near. By the way, I think I'll keep my bait in front of me from now on.

> PRAYER: Lord, I want to be clean today. Please forgive me for little things like _____. Please come soon, Lord Jesus. Amen.

---

[a] Third beatitude of Revelation.

The Historic Church

The steeple is a familiar part of the city skyline. The paint is antique white, a reminder that it was built over two-hundred years ago. You can buy a postcard inside at the guide's desk. The pipe organ was donated by a prominent member years ago. The music committee was careful to hire an organist with proper credentials. He plays only the best in sacred music. A plaque in the foyer lists the famous preachers who called this place home. They preached from the same Bible that is on pulpit today. Sermons on philosophy, literature, and social issues are advertised in the religion section of the newspaper. The pews used to be filled by the leading families of the community. Now, there is plenty of room.

Jesus had a message for the historic church. Read the letter to Sardis.

Revelation 3:1–6 (HCSB)

---

1 "Write to the angel of the church in Sardis:

"The One who has the seven spirits of God and the seven stars says: I know your works; you have a reputation for being alive, but you are dead. 2 Be alert and strengthen what remains, which is about to die, for I have not found your works complete before My God. 3 Remember, therefore, what you have received and heard; keep it, and repent. But if you are not alert, I will come like a thief, and you have no idea at what hour I will come against you. 4 But you have a few people in Sardis who have not defiled their clothes, and they will walk with Me in white, because they are worthy. 5 In the same way, the victor will be dressed in white clothes, and I will never erase his name from the book of life but will acknowledge his name before My Father and before His angels.

6 "Anyone who has an ear should listen to what the Spirit says to the churches.

Jesus knew all about the church in Sardis. He held the church in his hand for close inspection. He saw all that was happening, and all that was not happening. Sardis had a distinguished reputation, but hardly any spiritual life remained under the thin veneer of respectability.

When we first met Jesus, many of us had an exciting conversion, enthusiasm for the sharing the gospel, and an unquenchable thirst for the Bible. Now, we do what's expected, testify only about "back when ..." and dust the Bible on the coffee table. Perhaps, we have become like Sardis.

Jesus advised them to wake up, to remember what they had been taught, and to repent from their apathy. Jesus warned that if they did not repent, his coming would surprise them like a thief at night. Jesus was referring to this illustration.

> But know this: If the homeowner had known what time the thief was coming, he would have stayed alert and not let his house be

broken into. This is why you also must be ready, because the Son of Man is coming at an hour you do not expect.
>> Matthew 24:43–44 (HCSB)

A burglar broke into my neighbor's home, while they were out for the evening. When they returned, they were shocked to find the house had been carefully searched for valuables. Evidently, the burglar also was shocked by their return; they found an unfinished bottle of Coke on the kitchen table. Jesus will return unexpectedly, too.

> Besides this, knowing the time, it is already the hour for you to wake up from sleep, for now our salvation is nearer than when we first believed. The night is nearly over, and the daylight is near, so let us discard the deeds of darkness and put on the armor of light. Let us walk with decency, as in the daylight: not in carousing and drunkenness; not in sexual impurity and promiscuity; not in quarreling and jealousy. But put on the Lord Jesus Christ, and make no plans to satisfy the fleshly desires.
>> Romans 13:11–14 (HCSB)

Being prepared for Jesus to return means living a godly life, rather than doing whatever we want. Note that the symptoms of selfishness include not only worldly parties, but also jealousy and quarreling. Too often Christians accept jealousy and quarreling as normal, but Jesus wants these put aside, just like immorality and promiscuity. To *put on the Lord Jesus Christ* means to adopt his lifestyle in action, and to be like him in attitude.

A few in Sardis had maintained their spiritual life without any encouragement from the others. Jesus commended them for their pure lifestyle. He promised to walk with them, and to clothe them with his righteousness. This same promise is available to us, if we will follow their example. The others were clothed with the rags of their own respectability.[22]

FOR PERSONAL STUDY
Sardis   (3:1–6)

1. What is meant by a church being *dead* or *alive*? What are the symptoms of a dead church?

2. Which qualities of Jesus are referred to in verse 1? How does this picture of Jesus relate to the situation at Sardis?

3. What techniques are usually tried to enliven a dead church?

4. What cure for a dead church does Jesus give?

5. Are you a member of a Christian group that is like Sardis? How is it similar? How is it different?

---

[22] Isaiah 64:6.

The Obscure Church

A little church in the Andes Mountains is unseen by TV cameras. Events there don't make the front page. Even though their problems may seem insignificant to the rest of the world, they are very important to God. Rebel forces attacked a church meeting in Santa Rosa, Peru, killing seven people and wounding fourteen.[23] A few days later in Callqui, Peru, government troops entered a church looking for a suspect. When they failed to find him, they marched six men outside and shot them while the congregation was forced to sing. A leader of a Peruvian missionary movement said at that time, "Please pray for Peru. Its problems are increasing. Guerrilla warfare is spreading to many parts of the Andes, and Christians have been killed for not cooperating with them. Yet, these areas are experiencing a great awakening in the churches, and great numbers of the unsaved are seeking the Lord, including police and guerrillas."

Jesus had a message for the obscure church. Read the letter to Philadelphia.

Revelation 3:7–13 (HCSB)

---

7 "Write to the angel of the church in Philadelphia:

"The Holy One, the True One, the One who has the key of David, who opens and no one will close, and closes and no one opens says: 8 I know your works. Because you have limited strength, have kept My word, and have not denied My name, look, I have placed before you an open door that no one is able to close. 9 Take note! I will make those from the synagogue of Satan, who claim to be Jews and are not, but are lying—note this—I will make them come and bow down at your feet, and they will know that I have loved you. 10 Because you have kept My command to endure, I will also keep you from the hour of testing that is going to come over the whole world to test those who live on the earth. 11 I am coming quickly. Hold on to what you have, so that no one takes your crown. 12 The victor: I will make him a pillar in the sanctuary of My God, and he will never go out again. I will write on him the name of My God and the name of the city of My God—the new Jerusalem, which comes down out of heaven from My God—and My new name.

13 "Anyone who has an ear should listen to what the Spirit says to the churches.

Jesus has authority over God's household, the church. That authority is symbolized by the "key of David." In ancient times, the royal robe, the royal sash, and the keys to the palace were symbols of authority. For example, Isaiah said that Shebna, the palace administrator of Hezekiah, King of Judah, would

---

[23]*Christian Mission* (January–February 1985). Christian Aid Mission, Charlottsville, Virginia, provided reports from churches around the world through its magazine, *Christian Mission*. Christian Aid Mission is a non-denominational work supporting indigenous missions in poorer countries of the world.

be deposed, and that Eliakim would be promoted in his place. Speaking to Shebna, Isaiah prophesied,

> On that day I will call for my servant, Eliakim son of Hilkiah. I will clothe him with your robe and tie your sash around him. I will put your authority into his hand, and he will be like a father to the inhabitants of Jerusalem and to the House of Judah. I will place the key of the House of David on his shoulder; what he opens, no one can close; what he closes, no one can open.
>
> Isaiah 22:20–22 (HCSB)

Jesus has this kind of authority over the household of God. He will be like a father to the weak. He can make opportunities in unexpected places, and can foil the best laid plans.

The church in Philadelphia did not look like a success. They were not big and strong like Ephesus. They were second-class citizens of the local religious community. Instead of accomplishing great things for the kingdom of God, they just lived according to the Word, and remained loyal to Jesus. Jesus loved them.

The Andes mountain churches also had similar opportunities. Like the church in Smyrna, some even gave their lives for the gospel. Even though the Andes mountain churches seemed to be no match for guerrillas or soldiers, guns could not stop the gospel from spreading throughout the mountains. He gave them unique opportunities in the 1980s and 1990s.

Jesus promised to protect the church in Philadelphia from the disasters experienced by unbelievers.

> You will not fear the terror of the night, the arrow that flies by day, the plague that stalks in darkness, or the pestilence that ravages at noon. Though a thousand fall at your side and ten thousand at your right hand, the pestilence will not reach you. You will only see it with your eyes and witness the punishment of the wicked. Because you have made the Lord—my refuge, the Most High—your dwelling place, no harm will come to you; no plague will come near your tent.
>
> Psalms 91:5–10 (HCSB)

We can apply the promise to Philadelphia whenever fear and terror confront us. Even though life has many risks, we can go confidently from day to day when we live in the Lord's presence. Being close to the Lord is a safe place. He advised them to keep on living as they had been. He promised that those who overcome will always live in God's presence.

God didn't require the churches in the Andes Mountains to become famous and influential. He wanted them to overcome there in the mountains, spreading the gospel to neighbors, guerrillas, and soldiers.

FOR PERSONAL STUDY
Philadelphia (3:7–13)

1. Describe a modern church like Philadelphia.

2. What kind of troubles did Philadelphia have?

3. What was their outstanding virtue?

4. How are "opening doors" (verses 7–8) and being "a pillar in the temple" (verse 12) related to Jesus' promise to them?

5. What is the main idea of Jesus' message to Philadelphia?

6. Are you a member of a Christian group like Philadelphia? How is it similar? How is it different?

The Suburban Church

The community was a good place to raise a family. The lawns were all neatly trimmed. The commuter train station made it easy to get to work in the City. The church budget comfortably covered expenses. The pews were soft. The people were religious, but not too religious. The pastor was friendly. The sermon didn't quote the Bible much. There was no reason to get excited.

Jesus had a message for the suburban church. Read the letter to Laodicea.

Revelation 3:14–22 (HCSB)

---

14 "Write to the angel of the church in Laodicea:

"The Amen, the faithful and true Witness, the Originator of God's creation says: 15 I know your works, that you are neither cold nor hot. I wish that you were cold or hot. 16 So, because you are lukewarm, and neither hot nor cold, I am going to vomit you out of My mouth. 17 Because you say, 'I'm rich; I have become wealthy and need nothing,' and you don't know that you are wretched, pitiful, poor, blind, and naked, 18 I advise you to buy from Me gold refined in the fire so that you may be rich, white clothes so that you may be dressed and your shameful nakedness not be exposed, and ointment to spread on your eyes so that you may see. 19 As many as I love, I rebuke and discipline. So be committed and repent. 20 Listen! I stand at the door and knock. If anyone hears My voice and opens the door, I will come in to him and have dinner with him, and he with Me. 21 The victor: I will give him the right to sit with Me on My throne, just as I also won the victory and sat down with My Father on His throne.

22 "Anyone who has an ear should listen to what the Spirit says to the churches."

If the church at Laodicea had been enthusiastic, the Lord could have used them to spread the gospel. If they had been atheists, he could have sent the gospel to them. As it was, they were just religious enough to know all about the Christian life, without knowing the Christ himself.

Jesus was disgusted by their lukewarm attitude. As ruler of God's creation, he was not impressed by a bank account. Their true spiritual condition was wretched, pitiful, poor, blind, and naked. Jesus recommended that they turn to him for the solution.

He offered "gold," representing good works, such as giving to the poor. In the gospels, Jesus recommended storing this kind of treasure in heaven.[24] Similarly, Paul referred to works as either gold, silver, and costly stones, on the one hand, or wood, hay, and straw, on the other.[25]

Jesus offered "white garments," representing righteousness. At the wedding supper of the Lamb, the bride was dressed in white linen. "The fine linen is the righteousness of the saints."[26]

He offered "eye salve," to give sight to the spiritually blind, so they could discern their true spiritual condition. They were like the Pharisees whom Jesus confronted time after time.

> Blind guides! You strain out a gnat, yet gulp down a camel! Woe to you, scribes and Pharisees, hypocrites! You clean the outside of the cup and dish, but inside they are full of greed and self-indulgence! Blind Pharisee! First clean the inside of the cup, so the outside of it may also become clean.
>
> Matthew 23:24–26 (HCSB)

In prosperous times, it is easy to fall into the same attitudes as the Laodiceans had, concentrating on the superficial rather than true spirituality. "The new church is an architectural landmark of the community." "I'm so proud to have the bank president on our Board." "Look at the fancy dress Mrs. So-and-so is wearing today." "The teacher is so eloquent when he illustrates the lesson with literary references." A self-sufficient attitude is like a closed door to an intimate relationship with Jesus.

Jesus loves us. He's ready to help. He will befriend anyone who will repent. Those who do will sit with him as ruler of God's creation.

FOR PERSONAL STUDY
Laodicea   (3:14–22)

1. What were the problems in Laodicea?

2. What is meant by hot, cold, and lukewarm? Is it related to their economic status?

---

[24] Matthew 6:19–21 and Luke 12:33–34.
[25] 1 Corinthians 3:11–13.
[26] 19:8 (KJV).

3. What is meant by spiritual poverty, blindness, and nakedness?

4. How do the titles of Jesus in verse 14 relate to their situation?

5. What does Jesus' advice (verses 18–20) mean in practical terms for a modern church?

6. Are you a member of a Christian group that is like Laodicea? How is it similar? How is it different?

Review

Life always has hardships and obstacles, but Jesus is always with us to help us and to encourage us to be overcomers. Let us review chapters one through three of Revelation. John saw Jesus standing among seven lampstands, representing many kinds of local churches. We can apply these letters to local groups of Christians, with various strengths and weaknesses.

1. Ephesus, the Downtown Church, was industrious, but lacking their first love.

2. Smyrna, the Underground Church, was faithful, but suffering persecution.

3. Pergamum, the Permissive Church, was tolerant of false doctrine.

4. Thyatira, Reverend Jezebel's Church, was tolerant of corrupting leadership.

5. Sardis, the Historic Church, had a distinguished reputation, but was cold and dead in reality.

6. Philadelphia, the Obscure Church, was unknown but faithful.

7. Laodicea, the Suburban Church, was self confident, but lukewarm.

We can see many of these characteristics in ourselves as individuals, and in Christian groups, such as denominations, local churches, Sunday school classes, men's or women's groups, youth groups, campus Bible studies, and parachurch ministries. Each group has its own characteristics, and Jesus has advice for each. It may be a commendation, comfort, or call to repentance. Although every group faces problems, Jesus promises blessings to overcomers, and that includes us. Overcoming means obeying the advice of Jesus. Faith and obedience open the windows of heaven, supplying the power of God for a church to fulfill its destiny. The church must overcome.

> And they overcame [Satan] by the blood of the Lamb and by the word of their testimony, and they did not love their lives to the death.
>
> Revelation 12:11 (NKJV)

FOR PERSONAL STUDY
Review—Letters to Seven Churches (1:9–3:22)

1. List the features of the picture of Jesus in 1:9-20.

2. Make a table on a big sheet of paper. List each of the seven churches in the left column and make the following columns toward the right.

    - Picture of Jesus
    - Command
    - Fault or Problem
    - Warning
    - Promise

    Fill in the table with the characteristics of the seven churches.

3. What is the primary message to each church?

4. Make another table. In the left column, list some of the Christian groups to which you belong, for example, your local church, a Sunday School class, a men's group, a women's group, a youth group, a school club, or a community group. In two columns to the right list which of the seven churches fits your group the best, and the recommendation from Jesus for that church.

5. Which church does your personal life fit the best?

6. According to these letters, what does Jesus want for your life?

The Creator

Read Psalms 104:1–35.

> Worthy art Thou, our Lord and our God, to receive glory and honor and power; for Thou didst create all things, and because of Thy will they existed, and were created.
> Revelation 4:11 (NASB)

Creation declares the majesty of the Lord. The thunderstorm, the wind, and the lightening are his servants.

He arranges the tectonic plates to make room for the ocean, and puts sand on the beach to mark its boundary.

He provides fresh water for his creatures to drink. The water falls from the skies. Springs spout from the earth. Rivers flow to the sea.

He provides food for his creatures to to eat. Grass is for the cattle, crops for man, and prey for the lions.

He made the creatures of the sea, from tiny krill to great whales. He decorated the bottom with corals and sea anemones.

He planned the cycle of life, death, and birth. The Lord's works are amazing. I will sing of my Creator's glory and majesty all of my days.

PRAYER: O Lord God, when I see what you have made, all that I can do is humbly worship and praise you. Amen.

3

Creation Groans

> For we know that the whole creation has been groaning together with labor pains until now.
>
> Romans 8:22 (HCSB)

These are difficult times. The newspapers proclaim the violence, pollution, corruption, and suffering of our world. Terrorism, invasions, revolutions, military buildups, and war ravage various corners of the world. There is famine in Africa, an earthquake in Chile and another in Japan, a typhoon in the Philippines, and a flood in Bangladesh. The headlines go on and on. Our hearts ache for the poor and suffering. Not only are people victims, but the wild animals, birds and fish, and even the trees suffer as well. Creation is groaning. But there is hope. When Jesus returns, all creation will be freed from the curse of sin. There will be rejoicing instead of groaning.

John saw a scroll which was fastened with seven seals. Chapters 4 through 11 of Revelation tell us what happened as each seal was broken, and the scroll was unrolled.

As shown in the following outline, chapters 4 and 5 describe the scene in heaven and introduce the scroll. Then, one by one, the seals were broken; God's message was revealed. Chapter 6 describes the first six seals, but before the seventh seal was broken in chapter 8, there was an interlude in chapter 7. The vision of the seventh seal was itself made up of seven parts. Seven angels were each given a trumpet. Then one by one they sounded their trumpets; God's message was revealed. Chapters 8 and 9 describe the first six trumpets, but then, as with the seals, there was an interlude, followed by the last trumpet.

II. A Scroll with Seven Seals

Introduction	The Throne of God	4:1–5:14
1st Seal	A White Horse	6:1–2
2nd Seal	A Red Horse	6:3–4

Creation Groans

Illustration 3.1: A Throne in Heaven (4:1–11)

3rd Seal	A Black Horse	6:5–6
4th Seal	A Pale Horse	6:7–8
5th Seal	Martyrs	6:9–11
6th Seal	Upheaval	6:12–17
Interlude	Servants of God	7:1–17
7th Seal	Seven Trumpets	
Introduction	Incense	8:1–5
1st Trumpet	Trees	8:6–7
2nd Trumpet	Sea	8:8–9
3rd Trumpet	Rivers and Springs	8:10–11
4th Trumpet	Sun, Moon, Stars	8:12
5th Trumpet	Torment	8:13–9:11
6th Trumpet	Fire, Smoke, Sulfur	9:12–21
Interlude	My Witnesses	10:1–11:13
7th Trumpet	Christ Reigns	11:14–19

Holy, Holy, Holy

A throne. The dais is a few steps above the main floor in the House of Lords. An ornate chair is there, waiting. Only the monarch of England is allowed to sit there. Queen Elizabeth recently celebrated her ninetieth birthday. Each year, she speaks to Parliament from this throne.

God speaks to us from his throne in heaven. Read chapter 4 of Revelation.

Revelation 4:1–11 (HCSB)

> 1 After this I looked, and there in heaven was an open door. The first voice that I had heard speaking to me like a trumpet said, "Come up here, and I will show you what must take place after this."
> 2 Immediately I was in the Spirit, and a throne was set there in heaven. One was seated on the throne, 3 and the One seated looked like jasper and carnelian stone. A rainbow that looked like an emerald surrounded the throne. 4 Around that throne were 24 thrones, and on the thrones sat 24 elders dressed in white clothes, with gold crowns on their heads. 5 Flashes of lightning and rumblings of thunder came from the throne. Seven fiery torches were burning before the throne, which are the seven spirits of God. 6 Something like a sea of glass, similar to crystal, was also before the throne. Four living creatures covered with eyes in front and in back were in the middle and around the throne. 7 The first living creature was

like a lion; the second living creature was like a calf; the third living creature had a face like a man; and the fourth living creature was like a flying eagle. 8 Each of the four living creatures had six wings; they were covered with eyes around and inside. Day and night they never stop, saying:

> Holy, holy, holy,
> Lord God, the Almighty,
> who was, who is, and who is coming.

9 Whenever the living creatures give glory, honor, and thanks to the One seated on the throne, the One who lives forever and ever, 10 the 24 elders fall down before the One seated on the throne, worship the One who lives forever and ever, cast their crowns before the throne, and say:

> 11 Our Lord and God,
> You are worthy to receive
> glory and honor and power,
> because You have created all things,
> and because of Your will
> they exist and were created.

John saw a throne in heaven, the awesome presence of Almighty God. Twenty-four elders and four creatures worshiped around the throne.

In biblical times, elders were the leaders of the community. Each village had elders; the nation of Israel had elders; each church had elders. In this scene, the leaders of God's people worshiped before the throne of God.

Why were there twenty-four elders, rather than twenty-three, twelve, seven or some other number? Many commentators point out that twenty-four is the number of the twelve tribes of Israel plus the twelve apostles, signifying that saints from both Old Testament and New Testament eras are represented before the throne. The number twenty-four has another significance as well. King David appointed twenty-four chief men (elders) of Aaron's descendants to lead the priests serving in the temple.[1] Here in John's vision, we see twenty-four leaders serving at the throne of God.

We can feel the atmosphere of worship in God's presence. We too, as believers, are a priesthood whose function is to praise him. We can sing with the elders "Thou art worthy," praising the Lord because he is our maker.

Four creatures also worshiped around the throne. The word translated *beast* in the King James Version means simply any living creature.[2] These creatures were each like a different kind of animal (including mankind). Creation is part of God's royal entourage.

In the book of Ezekiel, chapters 1 and 10, there are similar visions of four living creatures around God's throne. These scriptures surely came to mind as

---

[1] 1 Chronicles 24:1–19, especially v.4.
[2] The Greek word *zōon* (*Strong's* No. 2198).

the first century Christians read this passage. So, when reading Revelation 4, we can meditate on the majesty of the associated scenes in Ezekiel's visions. We can sing with the four creatures, "Holy, Holy, Holy, Lord God Almighty."

Isaiah also saw the throne of God.

> Then I said: Woe is me for I am ruined because I am a man of unclean lips and live among a people of unclean lips, and because my eyes have seen the King, the Lord of Hosts.
>
> Isaiah 6:5 (HCSB)

Isaiah recognized his own sin and repented. After being cleansed by God, he was available for service. "Here am I. Send me!"[3] Just like Isaiah, when I see the majesty of my creator in Revelation 4, I can't continue just doing my own thing. After I turn from the sin in my life, I can say "Here am I. Send me!"

A scroll. When I opened the mailbox, an envelope was lying there with wax on the back. I knew that no one else had read the letter. It was still sealed. Upon closer inspection, one could see that someone had pressed a pattern into the hot wax. A signet ring is designed for this purpose. There was only one person in the world who had a signet ring with that pattern. I knew who the letter was from.

A sealed scroll had God's message to us. Read chapter 5 of Revelation.

Revelation 5:1–14 (HCSB)

> 1 Then I saw in the right hand of the One seated on the throne a scroll with writing on the inside and on the back, sealed with seven seals. 2 I also saw a mighty angel proclaiming in a loud voice, "Who is worthy to open the scroll and break its seals?" 3 But no one in heaven or on earth or under the earth was able to open the scroll or even to look in it. 4 And I cried and cried because no one was found worthy to open the scroll or even to look in it.
>
> 5 Then one of the elders said to me, "Stop crying. Look! The Lion from the tribe of Judah, the Root of David, has been victorious so that He may open the scroll and its seven seals." 6 Then I saw One like a slaughtered lamb standing between the throne and the four living creatures and among the elders. He had seven horns and seven eyes, which are the seven spirits of God sent into all the earth. 7 He came and took the scroll out of the right hand of the One seated on the throne.
>
> 8 When He took the scroll, the four living creatures and the 24 elders fell down before the Lamb. Each one had a harp and gold bowls filled with incense, which are the prayers of the saints. 9 And they sang a new song:

---

[3]Isaiah 6:8 (NASB).

> You are worthy to take the scroll
> and to open its seals,
> because You were slaughtered,
> and You redeemed people
> for God by Your blood
> from every tribe and language
> and people and nation.
> 10 You made them a kingdom
> and priests to our God,
> and they will reign on the earth.

11 Then I looked and heard the voice of many angels around the throne, and also of the living creatures and of the elders. Their number was countless thousands, plus thousands of thousands. 12 They said with a loud voice:

> The Lamb who was slaughtered is worthy
> to receive power and riches
> and wisdom and strength
> and honor and glory and blessing!

13 I heard every creature in heaven, on earth, under the earth, on the sea, and everything in them say:

> Blessing and honor and glory and dominion
> to the One seated on the throne,
> and to the Lamb, forever and ever!

14 The four living creatures said, "Amen," and the elders fell down and worshiped.

Chapter 4 sets the stage. Chapter 5 introduces a scroll fastened with seven seals. It was sealed in such a way that one could break an outer seal, and unroll it until stopped by the next seal. Thus, the scroll revealed its message bit by bit as each seal was broken.

In the ancient world, wax seals were used to prevent people from reading a letter that didn't belong to them. Only someone with the proper authority was permitted to break a seal. In John's vision, there was a problem; no one had the proper authority to open the seven-sealed scroll.

But then John saw a lamb who was worthy to open the scroll. All heaven worshiped the lamb. The passage includes three hymns to the lamb so that we can join in their worship.[4] In later chapters, we will discover what the scroll said, but this chapter focuses on the person authorized to open the scroll.

There can be no doubt that the Lamb of God is Jesus. John the Baptist saw Jesus and said "Behold, the Lamb of God!"[5] The titles *Lion of Judah*[6] and *Root*

---

[4] 5:9–10, 5:12, and 5:13.
[5] John 1:36 (KJV).
[6] Genesis 49:9–10.

of David[7] belong to the Messiah as well.

The first hymn explains the source of Jesus' authority to open the scroll. He is worthy to break the seals because he died for us on the cross. His authority as king, "the Lion of Judah," is founded on his mission as savior, "the Lamb of God." His redemption is available not only to you and me, but to every family, language group, ethnic group, and nationality. Jesus died for the sins of whole world, without discrimination. To reign with him, we must repent and accept the fact that he died for our sins and rose again.

In the first hymn, the beasts and the elders around the throne worshiped Jesus for what he has done. In the second hymn, the circle of praise widened. All of the angels in heaven worshiped him with royal honors. In the third hymn, all of creation joined the song, worshiping God the Creator, who sits on the throne, and Jesus the Redeemer, who is in the middle of the throne.

You and I can join the heavenly throng in praise and worship as we meditate on what Jesus did for us and on who he is. He died for our sins, and he rose from the dead as king of the universe.

FOR PERSONAL STUDY
The Throne of God   (4:1–5:14)

1. Compare this passage in several translations to get a clear picture of the scene. Describe the picture in your own words.

2. Why is God being praised?

3. What does the presence of the four creatures and the twenty-four elders emphasize in the picture?

4. What kind of feeling does the picture convey?

5. What is emphasized about Jesus in 5:1–7?

6. What is the main idea of the first hymn? (5:9–10)

7. What role of Jesus is emphasized in the second hymn? (5:12)

8. What is emphasized about Jesus in the third hymn? (5:13)

9. What kind of feeling does chapter 5 convey?

10. Paraphrase 5:9–10 in your own words. Each time it refers to *us*, substitute your own name.

11. Imagine yourself there next to John. Sing the hymn "Holy Holy Holy, Lord God Almighty." Meditate on the words of the song.[8]

---
[7] Isaiah 11:1.
[8] Lyrics by Reginald Heber.

Illustration 3.2: Four Horsemen (6:1–8)

Holy, Holy, Holy, Lord God Almighty!
Early in the morning our song shall rise to Thee;
Holy, Holy, Holy! Merciful and Mighty!
God in Three persons, blessed Trinity!

Holy, Holy, Holy! All the saints adore Thee,
Casting down their golden crowns around the glassy sea;
Cherubim and seraphim falling down before Thee,
Who wert, and art, and evermore shalt be.

Holy, Holy, Holy! Tho' the darkness hide Thee,
Tho' the eye of sinful man Thy glory may not see,
Only Thou art holy; there is none beside Thee
Perfect in power, in love, and purity.

Holy, Holy, Holy, Lord God Almighty!
All Thy works shall praise Thy name, in earth, and sky, and sea;
Holy, Holy, Holy! Merciful and Mighty!
God in Three persons, blessed Trinity!

FOR PERSONAL STUDY
The Lamb   (Isaiah 52:14–53:12)

Chapter 5 of Revelation pictures Jesus as the "Lamb that was slain." Read Isaiah 52:14–53:12.

1. List the feelings experienced by Jesus mentioned in this passage.

2. How does this passage say he reacted to the situation?

3. How does the death of Jesus fit into God's plan?

4. What should be our response to what Jesus has done?

5. Sing a hymn about Jesus dying for us, such as "The Old Rugged Cross."

Horsemen and More

In 1498, Albrecht Dürer published a set of woodcut prints illustrating Revelation. The text of Revelation was printed on the back of each print, making the set a picture book. The Apocalypse prints quickly became bestsellers at fairs throughout Europe.[9] The most famous of these is Four Horsemen, which depicts the opening verses of chapter 6.

Read chapter 6 of Revelation.

---

[9]Francis Russell, *The World of Dürer* (New York: Time-Life Books, 1967), pp. 66–69. Fourteen of the prints illustrate this book, courtesy of the Wetmore Print Collection at Connecticut College.

Revelation 6:1–17 (HCSB)

---

1 Then I saw the Lamb open one of the seven seals, and I heard one of the four living creatures say with a voice like thunder, "Come!" 2 I looked, and there was a white horse. The horseman on it had a bow; a crown was given to him, and he went out as a victor to conquer.

3 When He opened the second seal, I heard the second living creature say, "Come!" 4 Then another horse went out, a fiery red one, and its horseman was empowered to take peace from the earth, so that people would slaughter one another. And a large sword was given to him.

5 When He opened the third seal, I heard the third living creature say, "Come!" And I looked, and there was a black horse. The horseman on it had a set of scales in his hand. 6 Then I heard something like a voice among the four living creatures say, "A quart of wheat for a denarius, and three quarts of barley for a denarius—but do not harm the olive oil and the wine."

7 When He opened the fourth seal, I heard the voice of the fourth living creature say, "Come!" 8 And I looked, and there was a pale green horse. The horseman on it was named Death, and Hades was following after him. Authority was given to them over a fourth of the earth, to kill by the sword, by famine, by plague, and by the wild animals of the earth.

9 When He opened the fifth seal, I saw under the altar the people slaughtered because of God's word and the testimony they had. 10 They cried out with a loud voice: "Lord, the One who is holy and true, how long until You judge and avenge our blood from those who live on the earth?" 11 So a white robe was given to each of them, and they were told to rest a little while longer until the number would be completed of their fellow slaves and their brothers, who were going to be killed just as they had been.

12 Then I saw Him open the sixth seal. A violent earthquake occurred; the sun turned black like sackcloth made of goat hair; the entire moon became like blood; 13 the stars of heaven fell to the earth as a fig tree drops its unripe figs when shaken by a high wind; 14 the sky separated like a scroll being rolled up; and every mountain and island was moved from its place.

15 Then the kings of the earth, the nobles, the military commanders, the rich, the powerful, and every slave and free person hid in the caves and among the rocks of the mountains. 16 And they said to the mountains and to the rocks, "Fall on us and hide us from the face of the One seated on the throne and from the wrath of the Lamb, 17 because the great day of Their wrath has come! And who is able to stand?"

Horsemen and More   6:1–17

The Lamb opened the seals one by one, and John saw a vision for each one depicting the message of the scroll. When the first four seals were opened John saw horsemen. When the fifth seal was opened John saw the souls of martyrs, waiting for God to avenge their deaths. When the sixth seal was opened there were signs in nature.

Four seals. The first four seals are a group. As each seal was opened, a different colored horse with its rider appeared. These are Dürer's "Four Horsemen," from right to left.

The key word for the first horseman is *conquer*. When one country invades another, it usually means oppression and perhaps even genocide. History gives us many examples of the injustices suffered by conquered peoples.

The second horseman had a sword. This weapon of war has come to symbolize war itself. War not only means death for soldiers and civilians, but also grieving by families and wholesale destruction.

The third horseman had scales with which to measure out food. A voice announced prices for staples, "A quart of wheat for a denarius."[10] A quart of wheat flour doesn't make much bread. A *denarius* was a small silver Roman coin which was a day's wage for a laborer. At today's minimum wage in the United States for a day, that little bit of bread was pretty expensive. The common people were starving, but the rich, who used oil and wine, had plenty.

The fourth horseman brought death. The abode of the dead, Hades, followed the horseman. Together they used war, famine, disease, and predators to claim lives. These plagues are mentioned as a group throughout the Old Testament. The prophets condemned Israel for her idolatry, warning of these plagues.[11] This list of plagues is so common in Scripture that readers of Revelation should immediately be reminded of how Israel's sin resulted in war, famine, pestilence, and desolation.

The imagery of horsemen was not new with John's vision. Zechariah's vision used the same horses to depict the world situation after Israel's captivity.[12] Zechariah does not elaborate on the specific meaning of each horse, but John's explanation is quite clear: oppression, war, famine, and death. Application to our time is obvious. Just by reading the newspaper, we can see these four horsemen in action. These problems are rampant in our world today.

The fifth seal. When the fifth seal was opened, John saw martyrs for the faith eagerly waiting for that day when God's justice will prevail. Throughout the ages, faithful men and women have given their lives for the gospel. Chapter 11 of Hebrews recounts the faith of many Old Testament saints, including some who were martyred for their faith.

---

[10] 6:6 (NIV NOTES). The NIV translates the phrase as *a choenix of wheat*. A *choenix* was a unit of dry measure almost equal to a quart. K. Barker, *NIV Study Bible* (Grand Rapids, Michigan: Zondervan, 1995).

[11] Leviticus 26:21–26, Deuteronomy 32:24–25, Ezekiel 6:11–14.

[12] Zechariah 1:8–10 and Zechariah 6:1–3.

Illustration 3.3: The Fifth and Sixth Seals (6:9–17)

> They were stoned, they were sawed in two, they died by the sword, they wandered about in sheepskins, in goatskins, destitute, afflicted, and mistreated... All these were approved through their faith, but they did not receive what was promised.
>
> Hebrews 11:37–39 (HCSB)

They were willing to die without seeing the fulfillment of God's promises with their own eyes, but they knew that God is faithful. They were eager to see it, but God doesn't go by our timetable.

> One day is with the Lord as a thousand years, and a thousand years as one day. The Lord is not slack concerning his promise, as some men count slackness; but is long-suffering to us-ward, not willing that any should perish, but that all should come to repentance.
>
> 2 Peter 3:8–9 (KJV)

He wants all to hear the gospel and to repent. Meanwhile in this evil world, some today are giving their lives for the faith. They will join the martyrs under the altar, waiting for their day of vindication.

The sixth seal. When the sixth seal was opened, the events in nature were awesome. The foundation of everyday life, the solid ground, was shaken. The most predictable event of life, sunrise in the morning, didn't happen. The inspiration of lovers, the moon, was tainted. The astrologer's signs and the navigator's guide, the stars, were no longer there. Familiar landmarks, mountains on land and islands in the sea, moved to unknown places. Today, earthquakes, solar eclipses, lunar eclipses, meteors, landslides, and volcanos are local signs to us. All the reliable things in life can fail.

Interpreting the seals. We don't have to guess the significance of the signs. Revelation 6:15–17 tells us. The important people of this world knew what the visions of the seals meant. Ordinary people knew, too. They said that the king of the universe is angry, and he has a right to be angry.

The four horsemen depict consequences of sin that are rampant in our world today. Selfishness and greed cause oppression, war, economic chaos, and ultimately many deaths. Among those deaths are some of God's people, the martyrs for the faith. Signs in nature also make people realize that God's justice is coming.

Zechariah, who saw the same suffering, called on Israel to repent. " 'Return to Me,' says the Lord of hosts, 'and I will return to you.' "[13] We too should turn from the sin in our lives and toward the Lord.

> For the wrath of God is revealed from heaven against all ungodliness and unrighteousness of men, who hold the truth in unrighteousness.
>
> Romans 1:18 (KJV)

---

[13] Zechariah 1:3 (NKJV).

Illustration 3.4: Sealing God's Faithful (7:1–17)

The world's people knew of God's righteousness and wrath, and yet did not repent of their sin; instead, they wanted the mountains and rocks to fall on them. God is offering forgiveness and life to all who will turn toward him. The choice is clear: be crushed by sin, or receive forgiveness and life.

FOR PERSONAL STUDY
Six Seals   (6:1–17)

1. Read this chapter in a modern translation.

2. Summarize each of the first four seals (verses 1–8) in a single phrase.

3. Why did the martyrs in verses 9–11 cry out?

4. What was God's answer to them?

5. Do you have the same feelings as the martyrs in verses 9–11? Why?

6. List the signs mentioned with the Sixth Seal (verses 12–17). How would you feel if they happened all around you?

The Faithful

I had just signed the affidavit.[14] The notary public[15] squeezed the paper with her seal. The seal pressed a round raised pattern into the paper. Just to make sure it could be seen, she dusted the impression with black powder. My signature was now legally binding.

God put a seal on his faithful ones. Read chapter 7 of Revelation.

Revelation 7:1–17 (HCSB)

> 1 After this I saw four angels standing at the four corners of the earth, restraining the four winds of the earth so that no wind could blow on the earth or on the sea or on any tree. 2 Then I saw another angel, who had the seal of the living God rise up from the east. He cried out in a loud voice to the four angels who were empowered to harm the earth and the sea: 3 "Don't harm the earth or the sea or the trees until we seal the slaves of our God on their foreheads." 4 And I heard the number of those who were sealed:
>
> 144,000 sealed from every tribe of the Israelites:
> 5 12,000 sealed from the tribe of Judah,
> 12,000 from the tribe of Reuben,
> 12,000 from the tribe of Gad,
> 6 12,000 from the tribe of Asher,

---
[14] A legal document.
[15] In the United States, a notary public is a civil official who certifies signatures.

Illustration 3.5: The Lamb of God (7:9-17)

The Faithful 7:1–17

> 12,000 from the tribe of Naphtali,
> 12,000 from the tribe of Manasseh,
> 7 12,000 from the tribe of Simeon,
> 12,000 from the tribe of Levi,
> 12,000 from the tribe of Issachar,
> 8 12,000 from the tribe of Zebulun,
> 12,000 from the tribe of Joseph,
> 12,000 sealed from the tribe of Benjamin.

9 After this I looked, and there was a vast multitude from every nation, tribe, people, and language, which no one could number, standing before the throne and before the Lamb. They were robed in white with palm branches in their hands. 10 And they cried out in a loud voice:

> Salvation belongs to our God,
> who is seated on the throne,
> and to the Lamb!

11 All the angels stood around the throne, the elders, and the four living creatures, and they fell facedown before the throne and worshiped God, 12 saying:

> Amen! Blessing and glory and wisdom
> and thanksgiving and honor
> and power and strength
> be to our God forever and ever. Amen.

13 Then one of the elders asked me, "Who are these people robed in white, and where did they come from?"

14 I said to him, "Sir, you know."

Then he told me:

> These are the ones coming out of the great tribulation.
> They washed their robes and made them white
> in the blood of the Lamb.
> 15 For this reason they are before the throne of God,
> and they serve Him day and night in His sanctuary.
> The One seated on the throne will shelter them:
> 16 They will no longer hunger;
> they will no longer thirst;
> the sun will no longer strike them,
> nor will any heat.
> 17 For the Lamb who is at the center of the throne
> will shepherd them;
> He will guide them to springs of living waters,
> and God will wipe away every tear from their eyes.

In the sixth chapter we saw a complete description of what happened when the sixth seal was broken. Looking ahead, the eighth chapter begins with breaking the seventh seal. The seventh chapter is nestled among the visions of the seals to show how God cares for us.

Winds all over the Earth were about to blow. These were not just gentle breezes; they were gales, hurricanes, and tornadoes. Just in time, the angels held back the winds until God's servants on Earth were sealed. An angel had a signet which made an impression on each one's forehead. This showed that each belonged to God, like a notarized signature.

In Ezekiel, chapter 9, those who were faithful to the Lord were marked on the forehead, so that they would not be touched by angels of death.[16] Similarly, in Revelation 7 the winds were about to implement God's judgment, but first, God's people needed to be identified. The angel systematically sealed twelve thousand from each tribe of Israel.

Commentators have many different interpretations of the 144 thousand. I tried to figure out why the tribes of Israel were listed in this specific order. Was there some deep hidden truth in the order of the names? However, by focusing on such details, I was missing the main point. God marks his people, regardless of the order listed.

The entire nation of Israel consisted of the twelve tribes, so some from each tribe were sealed. Irrespective of one's specific interpretation of the 144,000, we can apply the idea of sealing to all of God's servants.

> When you heard the message of truth, the gospel of your salvation, and when you believed in Him, you were also sealed with the promised Holy Spirit. He is the down payment of our inheritance, for the redemption of the possession, to the praise of His glory.
> Ephesians 1:13–14 (HCSB)

We who believe are marked by the Holy Spirit who lives in us. Just as the angel with the signet marked each of God's servants, the Holy Spirit marks us. The Lord is patient, waiting for us to repent.[17] He held back destruction of this world so that I could believe in him. God knows that I belong to him, just like the 144 thousand.

The scene changes in the middle of chapter 7 from Earth to heaven. John saw a great multitude, the angels, the elders and the four creatures praising God together. We have seen the angels, the elders and the four creatures around God's throne before. But who is this multitude? Why are they praising him?

The passage identifies the great multitude; they are Christians coming "out of the great tribulation."[18] The word translated *tribulation* means pressure or affliction.[19] This great multitude in heaven is like the church in Smyrna, overcomers in the face of great affliction. Those who had suffered for their faith

---

[16] Ezekiel 9:4.
[17] 2 Peter 3:9.
[18] 7:14 (KJV).
[19] Vine, *s.v. tribulation*.

praised God for his wonderful salvation. Jesus is the Lamb of God, who died on the cross for us. The rest of heaven said, "Amen," agreeing with the multitude's hymn and adding praise of their own.

The passage describes what it is like to live in the presence of the Lord. Heat, hunger, and thirst are not problems. He gives us life like a shepherd gives water to his flock. He comforts us. We rejoice because we are with him.

Even though we aren't in heaven yet, we can still have hearts full of worship for him. We can worship with the heavenly multitude, praising him for our salvation, agreeing with the rest of heaven that blessing, glory, wisdom, thanksgiving, honor, power, and might belong to our God, and thanking him for his presence.

FOR PERSONAL STUDY
Servants of God (7:1–17)

1. What would the winds have done if they hadn't been held back?
2. What was the relationship to God of those who were sealed?
3. Why did the great multitude praise God?
4. What did the heavenly host say in praise?
5. What are God's promises to the great multitude?
6. Paraphrase the promises in your own words. Each time a promise refers to *them*, substitute your own name.

Bugle Calls

The vision of the seventh seal followed the pattern of the entire scroll. A scene in heaven introduced seven trumpets, followed by scenes on Earth as each trumpet sounded. After sounding six trumpets, God still wanted mankind to repent. God has patiently waited for mankind to turn away from sin. He is offering something much better, but mankind will not repent. The following outline shows the structure of these chapters.

7th Seal	Seven Trumpets	
Introduction	Incense	8:1–5
1st Trumpet	Trees	8:6–7
2nd Trumpet	Sea	8:8–9
3rd Trumpet	Rivers and Springs	8:10–11
4th Trumpet	Sun, Moon, Stars	8:12
5th Trumpet	Torment	8:13–9:11
6th Trumpet	Fire, Smoke, Sulfur	9:12–21

Illustration 3.6: Trumpets (8:1–12)

Interlude	My Witnesses	10:1–11:13
7th Trumpet	Christ Reigns	11:14–19

When the seventh seal was broken, there was silence in heaven. There was no singing, no "Hallelujah," no "Amen," just silence. Something had to be done about the mess on Earth. Seven trumpets were given to angels, ready for his command. The first four trumpets are a group like the first four seals were a group. As each of the first four trumpets was sounded, something burning fell from heaven, and creation suffered. The last three trumpets are also a group; each is called a *woe*.[20] As the fifth and sixth trumpets sounded, men suffered instead of creation. When the seventh trumpet sounded, God's power became obvious.

Incense

The altar of incense in the Holy Place of the Tabernacle was small and covered with gold. Sweet spices were burned on it during daily prayer.[21] This physical furniture was merely an imitation of what John saw in heaven.[22]

Read this section's Scripture passage.

Revelation 8:1–5 (HCSB)

> 1 When He opened the seventh seal, there was silence in heaven for about half an hour. 2 Then I saw the seven angels who stand in the presence of God; seven trumpets were given to them. 3 Another angel, with a gold incense burner, came and stood at the altar. He was given a large amount of incense to offer with the prayers of all the saints on the gold altar in front of the throne. 4 The smoke of the incense, with the prayers of the saints, went up in the presence of God from the angel's hand. 5 The angel took the incense burner, filled it with fire from the altar, and hurled it to the earth; there were rumblings of thunder, flashes of lightning, and an earthquake.

Prayers of the saints went up to God from the heavenly altar of incense. Our prayers go up to God like sweet smelling incense. Even when we don't know what to say, the Holy Spirit intercedes for us according to the will of God.[23] Our prayers are important to him. Just as the Old Testament priests offered the incense for the people in the Tabernacle, Jesus is now a priest for us in the heavenly Tabernacle. Our prayers are answered because of him. We can come boldly to the God of the universe in prayer.

---

[20] 8:13, 9:12, and 11:14.
[21] Exodus 30:1–8.
[22] Hebrews 8:1–2.
[23] Romans 8:27.

Let us therefore come boldly unto the throne of grace, that we may obtain mercy, and find grace to help in time of need.

> Hebrews 4:16 (KJV)

After the prayers went up, the angel at the altar threw fire to the Earth. The action began.

FOR PERSONAL STUDY
Incense (8:1–5)

1. Review the description of the altar of incense in Exodus 30:1–8.

2. When was Aaron supposed to burn incense and what did God promise he would do? (Exodus 30:6–8)

3. Why do you suppose prayer "smells good" to God?

4. Spend some time in prayer. Include several kinds of prayer, using each phrase of the model prayer that Jesus taught us as a starting point, and then praying over areas of your own life.

> Our Father which art in heaven,
> Hallowed be thy name.
> Thy kingdom come.
> Thy will be done in earth, as it is in heaven.
> Give us this day our daily bread.
> And forgive us our debts,
> As we forgive our debtors.
> And lead us not into temptation,
> But deliver us from evil:
> For thine is the kingdom, and the power, and the glory,
> for ever.
> Amen.
>
> Matthew 6:9–13 (KJV)

Catastrophes

When I was in the army, the blast of a bugle was the first thing I heard in the morning. The sound of reveille meant it was time to get going for the day. In the days before walkie-talkie radios, bugle calls were used in battle to give commands to the troops. The sound of the distant bugle would cut through the noise. Everyone would know what to do. Just as each bugle call had a specific meaning in battle, God's bugle calls have specific meaning for us.

Bugle Calls   8:6–9:21

Four trumpets.   Read the remainder of chapter 8 of Revelation.

Revelation 8:6–12 (HCSB)

---

6 And the seven angels who had the seven trumpets prepared to blow them.

7 The first angel blew his trumpet, and hail and fire, mixed with blood, were hurled to the earth. So a third of the earth was burned up, a third of the trees were burned up, and all the green grass was burned up.

8 The second angel blew his trumpet, and something like a great mountain ablaze with fire was hurled into the sea. So a third of the sea became blood, 9 a third of the living creatures in the sea died, and a third of the ships were destroyed.

10 The third angel blew his trumpet, and a great star, blazing like a torch, fell from heaven. It fell on a third of the rivers and springs of water. 11 The name of the star is Wormwood, and a third of the waters became wormwood. So, many of the people died from the waters, because they had been made bitter.

12 The fourth angel blew his trumpet, and a third of the sun was struck, a third of the moon, and a third of the stars, so that a third of them were darkened. A third of the day was without light, and the night as well.

As each angel sounded his trumpet, God's message was revealed in events on Earth. Each blast of the trumpet was a bugle call announcing God's message.

When the first trumpet sounded, forest fires swept the land. One third of the trees and all the grass were burned.

When the second trumpet sounded, sea creatures great and small were killed. One third of the ocean became blood. Whales, fish, shrimp, and coral cannot live in coagulated blood. One third of ocean life died. Ships were destroyed, too.

When the third trumpet sounded, many people died from contaminated water. One third of the rivers and springs became poisonous. The pollution was called *Wormwood* which is a poisonous plant.[24]

When the fourth trumpet sounded, one third of the lights in the sky were darkened. One third of the sun's light, one third of the moon's light, and one third of the light of the stars was blocked.

The visions depicted events with global scope. God's message is for the whole world. When we see local disasters today, we are reminded of the trumpets in Revelation. Natural forest fires are caused by lightning strikes, "fire from heaven."[25] Sometimes such thunderstorms have hail as well. A forest fire

---

[24] Vine, *s.v. wormwood*. Jeremiah 9:15, Jeremiah 23:15, Lamentations 3:15, and Amos 5:7.
[25] Some forest fires are caused by human carelessness and arson.

Illustration 3.7: The Sixth Trumpet (9:13–19)

can devastate hundreds of square miles. The sea turned to blood reminds us of local red tides, where toxic red algae blooms clog the water, killing marine life. The bitter water is like drinking water poisoned by toxic chemicals or bacteria. When smog moves in you can't see the sun, moon, or stars. A volcanic eruption can spew great clouds of ash that circle the globe.

Whenever a natural disaster hits close to home, people realize how fragile life is. Forest fires can threaten where you live. Red tide devastates marine industries. Polluted drinking water can kill. Smog or ash can choke everyone. The devastation of natural disasters are reminders to take a close look at the patterns of our lives, and to repent wherever selfish thoughts and actions arise.

Woes. The dictionary says *woe* expresses grief, regret, or distress.[26] The angel proclaimed "Woe" to mankind because of the remaining trumpets. As the fifth and sixth trumpets sounded, men suffered instead of creation.

Read chapter 9 of Revelation.

Revelation 8:13–9:21 (HCSB)

> 13 I looked again and heard an eagle flying high overhead, crying out in a loud voice, "Woe! Woe! Woe to those who live on the earth, because of the remaining trumpet blasts that the three angels are about to sound!"
>
> 1 The fifth angel blew his trumpet, and I saw a star that had fallen from heaven to earth. The key to the shaft of the abyss was given to him. 2 He opened the shaft of the abyss, and smoke came up out of the shaft like smoke from a great furnace so that the sun and the air were darkened by the smoke from the shaft. 3 Then locusts came out of the smoke on to the earth, and power was given to them like the power that scorpions have on the earth. 4 They were told not to harm the grass of the earth, or any green plant, or any tree, but only people who do not have God's seal on their foreheads. 5 They were not permitted to kill them but were to torment them for five months; their torment is like the torment caused by a scorpion when it strikes a man. 6 In those days people will seek death and will not find it; they will long to die, but death will flee from them.
>
> 7 The appearance of the locusts was like horses equipped for battle. Something like gold crowns was on their heads; their faces were like men's faces; 8 they had hair like women's hair; their teeth were like lions' teeth; 9 they had chests like iron breastplates; the sound of their wings was like the sound of chariots with many horses rushing into battle; 10 and they had tails with stingers like scorpions, so that with their tails they had the power to harm people for five months. 11 They had as their king the angel of the abyss; his name

---

[26] *Webster's Seventh New Collegiate Dictionary* (Springfield, Massachusetts: G. & C. Merriam, 1969), s.v. *woe*.

in Hebrew is Abaddon, and in Greek he has the name Apollyon. 12 The first woe has passed. There are still two more woes to come after this.

13 The sixth angel blew his trumpet. From the four horns of the gold altar that is before God, I heard a voice 14 say to the sixth angel who had the trumpet, "Release the four angels bound at the great river Euphrates." 15 So the four angels who were prepared for the hour, day, month, and year were released to kill a third of the human race. 16 The number of mounted troops was 200 million; I heard their number. 17 This is how I saw the horses in my vision: The horsemen had breastplates that were fiery red, hyacinth blue, and sulfur yellow. The heads of the horses were like lions' heads, and from their mouths came fire, smoke, and sulfur. 18 A third of the human race was killed by these three plagues—by the fire, the smoke, and the sulfur that came from their mouths. 19 For the power of the horses is in their mouths and in their tails, for their tails, which resemble snakes, have heads, and they inflict injury with them.

20 The rest of the people, who were not killed by these plagues, did not repent of the works of their hands to stop worshiping demons and idols of gold, silver, bronze, stone, and wood, which are not able to see, hear, or walk. 21 And they did not repent of their murders, their sorceries, their sexual immorality, or their thefts.

When the fifth trumpet sounded, people who did not have the seal of God were tormented for five months. A star fell from heaven, who opened the "bottomless pit" (KJV). A plague of locusts came out of the pit which tormented mankind. This was not an ordinary star and they were not ordinary locusts.

Isaiah called Satan *Lucifer*, meaning shining one, a star.[27] Jesus said he saw Satan fall from heaven like lightning, and he described Satan's power as serpents and scorpions.[28] This parallels the star that John saw fall from heaven and which released locusts with tails like scorpions. Satan wants to torment mankind, the part of creation made in God's image. The locusts were allowed to attack only those who did not have the seal of God.

Today, a person who has not trusted in Jesus, is vulnerable to the overwhelming attack of Satan. His demons are like a swarm of locusts with scorpion tails, which can fill life with despair and thoughts of suicide. However, believers have the seal of God, the Holy Spirit. Jesus has given us authority over all the power of the enemy. Satan's power need not hurt us. It is very comforting to know that no matter what Satan tries to do, we have the power to resist him, to be firm in our faith, and to be victorious.[29] God puts the Holy

---

[27] Compare Isaiah 14:12 in KJV and NIV.
[28] Luke 10:18–19.
[29] 1 Peter 5:8–9.

Spirit in the one who turns to Jesus. The Holy Spirit is his seal of protection. He fills a believer with his love, joy, peace, and the power to overcome Satan.

When the sixth trumpet sounded, God ordered four angels to be released and with them a great army. The number of angels reminds us of the north, south, east, and west. This plague was worldwide. Their horses breathed fire, smoke, and burning sulfur, which killed one third of mankind.

We usually think of angels as good guys with white robes, wings, and harps. These angels were agents of death whom God had been restraining from their awful mission until this time.

In ancient times, the cavalry was the small elite part of an army, which could defeat a much larger infantry force. The army released with the four angels was intimidating. Not only did it have overwhelming numbers; it was all cavalry. The appearance of the horses was fierce. They had serpents for tails. This indicates the demonic nature of this army. Their mission was to kill one third of mankind with fire, smoke, and burning sulfur.

These remind us of local volcanic eruptions with hot lava flows that burn everything in their paths, ash clouds that can bury cities, choking everything that breathes, and sulfuric acid fumes that poison the air.

Interpreting the trumpets. The meaning of the trumpets is clear from the reaction of the world's peoples in 9:20–21. After the six trumpets had sounded, mankind did not repent, even though they saw many of their neighbors die. They continued to worship gods they made up, to murder, to seek the occult, to exploit sex, and to steal. These same things are rampant in our society today. These same things are listed in Paul's letter to the Galatians which says, "They which do such things shall not inherit the kingdom of God."[30] They rejected the same inheritance that God offers us.

Destruction and death permeate our world, today. God is offering righteousness and life through Jesus. God's trumpets are a signal to turn from sin and death, and to accept his gift.

> The wages of sin is death; but the gift of God is eternal life through Jesus Christ our Lord.
>
> Romans 6:23 (KJV)

FOR PERSONAL STUDY
Six Trumpets   (8:6–9:21)

1. What was destroyed at the sound of each of the first four trumpets?

2. What was the effect of the fifth trumpet on nonbelievers?

3. What was its effect on believers?

---

[30] Galatians 5:19–21 (KJV).

Illustration 3.8: A Bitter-Sweet Book (10:1-11)

Bugle Calls 10:1–11:13

4. Summarize the effect of the sixth trumpet?
5. What are modern examples of the sins listed in 9:20–21?

My Witnesses

At the close of the ninth chapter, we saw that mankind did not repent after six trumpets sounded announcing God's judgment against sin. In the latter part of chapter eleven we will see what happened when the seventh trumpet sounded. The passage between the visions of the sixth and seventh trumpets shows us our part in spreading God's message.

A little scroll.   Read chapter 10 of Revelation.

Revelation 10:1–11 (HCSB)

---

1 Then I saw another mighty angel coming down from heaven, surrounded by a cloud, with a rainbow over his head. His face was like the sun, his legs were like fiery pillars, 2 and he had a little scroll opened in his hand. He put his right foot on the sea, his left on the land, 3 and he cried out with a loud voice like a roaring lion. When he cried out, the seven thunders spoke with their voices. 4 And when the seven thunders spoke, I was about to write. Then I heard a voice from heaven, saying, "Seal up what the seven thunders said, and do not write it down!"

5 Then the angel that I had seen standing on the sea and on the land raised his right hand to heaven. 6 He swore an oath by the One who lives forever and ever, who created heaven and what is in it, the earth and what is in it, and the sea and what is in it: "There will no longer be an interval of time, 7 but in the days of the sound of the seventh angel, when he will blow his trumpet, then God's hidden plan will be completed, as He announced to His servants the prophets."

8 Now the voice that I heard from heaven spoke to me again and said, "Go, take the scroll that lies open in the hand of the angel who is standing on the sea and on the land."

9 So I went to the angel and asked him to give me the little scroll. He said to me, "Take and eat it; it will be bitter in your stomach, but it will be as sweet as honey in your mouth."

10 Then I took the little scroll from the angel's hand and ate it. It was as sweet as honey in my mouth, but when I ate it, my stomach became bitter. 11 And I was told, "You must prophesy again about many peoples, nations, languages, and kings."

John saw an angel with a book in his hand, a messenger from God's presence. The messenger is described in detail. He had a rainbow for a crown like

Bitter-Sweet

Read Psalms 19:7–11.

> And I took the little book out of the angel's hand and ate it, and it was in my mouth sweet as honey; and when I had eaten it, my stomach was made bitter. And they said to me, "You must prophesy again concerning many peoples and nations and tongues and kings."
> Revelation 10:10–11 (NASB)

I was surprised one day when a coworker started asking questions about my religion. The office was too busy, so we had lunch together. I was excited by the opportunity to share the gospel.

I found that she knew about Jesus, but she did not realize that he is God. Throughout the lunch hour, we looked at scriptures about Jesus, worship, and a personal relationship with him. The good news is sweet.

When lunch ended, I was sure she understood the gospel. But, she wasn't willing to commit her life. Not long afterward she changed jobs, and I lost touch.

It feels so good when I share the gospel with others. The gospel is indeed good news. Like the psalmist said, the Word of God tastes like honey. But when my message of good news is rejected, the disappointment is sharp and bitter.

Sharing the gospel is bitter-sweet. The gospel message is sweet, but rejection is bitter.

PRAYER: Dear God, I am willing to speak whether they listen or not. Amen.

the rainbow around God's throne.[31] His face was like the sun, just like the face of Jesus.[32] His feet were like fire; the feet of Jesus glowed like bronze in a fire.[33] His voice was like the Lion of Judah.[34] In other words, He looked like Jesus.

When he cried out, God answered him. God's voice is described as "thunder" in other scriptures such as at Mount Sinai and at the tomb of Lazarus.[35] Even though we are not told exactly what God said, it shows the closeness of Jesus and the Father.

The message is clearly stated: "There will be no more delay!"[36] The mystery of God will be fulfilled at the seventh trumpet. Paul explained the mystery to the Corinthians. Those who have not died when Jesus returns will be changed, "at the last trumpet."[37] Jesus will return with the sounding of the trumpet of God.[38] I'm expecting the personal return of Jesus anytime. This hope is both a comfort when the troubles of life press in, and an incentive to spread the gospel.

The angel gave John a scroll to eat. John was apparently surprised that it was both sweet and bitter. Ezekiel's vision also had a scroll which was both sweet and bitter as a symbol for God's message.[39] Ezekiel's message was filled with "lamentations, mourning and woe," because the nation of Israel was not willing to listen and repent.[40] Our message is bitter also, because the world is not willing to listen to the gospel and repent. The gospel is for the whole world. We are to make disciples everywhere. When we share about Jesus with neighbors and coworkers, we are living these verses. My wife and I know people from many ethnic backgrounds. We meet tourists, students, and immigrants from other countries. The jive of the street is a different language from that of the board room. Not only coworkers need to hear about Jesus, the boss does, too. The gospel is needed by people of all backgrounds, of all ethnicities, from all countries, no matter how they talk, and no matter how important their position.

Measurements. Read the first thirteen verses of chapter 11.

Revelation 11:1–13 (HCSB)

---

1 Then I was given a measuring reed like a rod, with these words: "Go and measure God's sanctuary and the altar, and count those who worship there. 2 But exclude the courtyard outside the sanctuary. Don't measure it, because it is given to the nations, and they

---

[31] 4:3.
[32] 1:16.
[33] 1:15.
[34] 5:5.
[35] Exodus 19:19 and John 12:28–30.
[36] 10:6 (NIV).
[37] 1 Corinthians 15:51–52.
[38] 1 Thessalonians 4:16.
[39] Ezekiel 2:8–3:3.
[40] Ezekiel 3:7.

will trample the holy city for 42 months. 3 I will empower my two witnesses, and they will prophesy for 1,260 days, dressed in sackcloth." 4 These are the two olive trees and the two lampstands that stand before the Lord of the earth. 5 If anyone wants to harm them, fire comes from their mouths and consumes their enemies; if anyone wants to harm them, he must be killed in this way. 6 These men have the power to close up the sky so that it does not rain during the days of their prophecy. They also have power over the waters to turn them into blood and to strike the earth with every plague whenever they want.

7 When they finish their testimony, the beast that comes up out of the abyss will make war with them, conquer them, and kill them. 8 Their dead bodies will lie in the public square of the great city, which prophetically is called Sodom and Egypt, where also their Lord was crucified. 9 And representatives from the peoples, tribes, languages, and nations will view their bodies for three and a half days and not permit their bodies to be put into a tomb. 10 Those who live on the earth will gloat over them and celebrate and send gifts to one another because these two prophets brought judgment to those who live on the earth.

11 But after three and a half days, the breath of life from God entered them, and they stood on their feet. So great fear fell on those who saw them. 12 Then they heard a loud voice from heaven saying to them, "Come up here." They went up to heaven in a cloud, while their enemies watched them. 13 At that moment a violent earthquake took place, a tenth of the city fell, and 7,000 people were killed in the earthquake. The survivors were terrified and gave glory to the God of heaven.

John was commanded to measure the sanctuary of the temple and the worshipers. Similarly, Ezekiel watched an angel measure the temple, the courtyards, and the walls inside and out.[41] After it was all measured, Ezekiel saw the glory of the Lord fill the sanctuary. Then the Lord called for Israel to repent, so that a holy God could live among them.

Ezekiel described the entire temple complex in detail, including walls, and courtyards. However, John was told to measure only the sanctuary, not the courtyard, because unbelievers will control it and its surroundings (Jerusalem) for three and a half years. In other words, the area outside the sanctuary will not be holy.

We can apply this picture to Christians today. Paul tells us that we are the sanctuary of the temple of God.[42] Similarly, Peter explains that believers are a spiritual house under construction.[43] Each Christian is a stone in the building.

---

[41] Ezekiel 40:1–43:12.
[42] 1 Corinthians 3:16.
[43] 1 Peter 2:5.

You and I live in a secular society. Our surroundings are not holy to the Lord, even though the Holy Spirit lives inside of us. We are the sanctuary of God, and we are its worshipers. The glory of the Lord can fill your life and my life just like it filled the sanctuary Ezekiel saw, even though we live in secular society.

John was told about two witnesses who preached to the whole world. They performed signs and wonders similar to those of Moses and Elijah. They continued for 1,260 days, which is about three and a half years. They were martyred. While their bodies lay dead in the streets of Jerusalem, the people of the world celebrated. After three and a half days, they were resurrected and went up into heaven. That stopped the party. People were terrified, and glorified God. Can you imagine the nightly news on TV? Let's look at some of the details of this story, and see what they mean and how they apply to our lives.

The two witnesses were wearing sackcloth. This indicates that their message was one of mourning and lamentation. Many of the Old Testament prophets wore sackcloth when they called for repentance in Israel. These two witnesses had a message of repentance.

The two witnesses are described as olive trees and as lampstands. John had already seen lampstands which represented local churches.[44] Zechariah had a vision of two olive trees and a lampstand.[45] Olive oil was used in the lamps of that time. In Zechariah's vision, the oil signified the Holy Spirit.[46] Zechariah saw clusters of olives emptying oil into the lampstand. He was told that they were literally "sons of fresh oil," in other words anointed ones. At the start of His ministry, Jesus read from Isaiah in the synagogue. "He anointed me to preach the gospel to the poor."[47] These two witnesses were anointed to preach, too.

Just like olive trees have oil, we have the Holy Spirit in us. Just like oil is the source of power for a lamp, the Holy Spirit is the source of light in our lives. We are anointed by the Holy Spirit to preach, too.

The two witnesses did signs which were similar to those done by Moses and Elijah. Elijah prayed and it didn't rain for three and a half years. Moses turned the water in Egypt into blood, and called down other plagues on Egypt.

James teaches that our prayers can accomplish much, just like Elijah's did.[48] We can witness with the same power as Moses and Elijah did.

When the appointed time came, the witnesses were martyred by the forces of evil. The world thought that their problems were over—no more prophets to bother them. To their surprise, the witnesses were resurrected and went up to heaven in a cloud. We too will be resurrected and go up in a cloud to be with the Lord.[49]

At that time, a great earthquake shook Jerusalem, and the world's people were terrified. Not only was the earthquake itself frightening, but they realized

---

[44] 1:20.
[45] Zechariah 4:1–14.
[46] Zechariah 4:6.
[47] Luke 4:16–21 (NASB).
[48] James 5:16–18.
[49] 1 Thessalonians 4:13–18.

The Almighty

Read 1 Kings 20:13–30.

> We thank You, Lord God, the Almighty, who is and who was, because You have taken Your great power and have begun to reign.
> Revelation 11:17 (HCSB)

Aram[a] was at war with Israel. Israel faced a vast army. Overwhelming odds were against them, but the Lord demonstrated his power, routing the army of Aram. The Arameans excused themselves saying, "Their gods are gods of the hills. But if we fight them on the plains, surely we will be stronger than they."[b] They thought the Lord stayed in one place. Aram lost the next battle in the valley, too.

As I was growing up, I enjoyed going to church. I knew the songs about "Lord God Almighty." When Monday morning came, I tried to solve my problems myself. I acted like God stayed inside the church building. But I found out that God answers my prayers on Mondays, too. Now I know that "Lord God Almighty" is not just lyrics in a song. I worship him every day because he is the Almighty, ruler of all heaven and Earth—even Monday mornings.

PRAYER: Dear God, I worship you because you are the Almighty and there is no one stronger than you. Amen.

---

[a] Aram was in modern Syria.
[b] 1 Kings 20:23 (NIV).

that the witnesses had been preaching the truth.

This interlude between the blasts of trumpets has emphasized witnessing for our Lord. He has a message for us. The message is sweet, but the world's rejection is bitter. We are the sanctuary of the Holy Spirit who gives us the power to be effective. Even if we are martyred, we will be resurrected when Jesus comes again. This is the life of a believer, a witness for Jesus.

FOR PERSONAL STUDY
My Witnesses   (10:1–11:13)

1. What is the main idea of the angel's proclamation?

2. Why was John told to eat the little book?

3. What qualities do sweet and bitter suggest?

4. Summarize what happened to the two witnesses.

5. How are the two witnesses similar to Moses and Elijah?

6. What is the main theme of the entire passage?

7. From among your acquaintances:
    - List their ethnic groups.
    - List their countries of birth.
    - List their native languages.
    - List those who are a "boss."

8. Put a check by the ones with whom you have already shared about Jesus, and note that you can look forward to sharing with the others.[50]

King of Kings

The President of the United States has the highest military rank, the Commander-in-Chief. A military band is usually present for official occasions at the White House. When the President comes in, the band plays "Hail to the Chief." When Jesus returns, I think the band will play the "Hallelujah Chorus."

Read the remainder of chapter 11 of Revelation.

> Revelation 11:14–19 (HCSB)
>
> 14 The second woe has passed. Take note: The third woe is coming quickly!
>
> 15 The seventh angel blew his trumpet, and there were loud voices in heaven saying:

---

[50] 10:11.

> The kingdom of the world has become the kingdom
> of our Lord and of His Messiah,
> and He will reign forever and ever!

16 The 24 elders, who were seated before God on their thrones, fell facedown and worshiped God, 17 saying:

> We thank You, Lord God, the Almighty,
> who is and who was,
> because You have taken Your great power
> and have begun to reign.
> 18 The nations were angry,
> but Your wrath has come.
> The time has come
> for the dead to be judged
> and to give the reward
> to Your servants the prophets,
> to the saints, and to those who fear Your name,
> both small and great,
> and the time has come to destroy
> those who destroy the earth.

19 God's sanctuary in heaven was opened, and the ark of His covenant appeared in His sanctuary. There were flashes of lightning, rumblings of thunder, an earthquake, and severe hail.

We recall that the last three trumpets were a group. The angel proclaimed "Woe" to mankind. This passage completes the trio of woes, introducing the seventh trumpet. The announcement of the seventh trumpet said that Jesus has authority over all the world and he will reign forever.

The elders in heaven worshiped God. That is exactly how we should react when we meditate on who Jesus is. He is the King of Kings and the Lord of Lords. The hymn of the elders describes the culmination of history. Jesus will judge the dead, reward his faithful, and destroy his enemies. Jesus will reign in power even though the nations of the world won't like it. The nations will think his reign is a "woe." The psalmist described the reaction of the nations. They will be angry, plotting and scheming to overthrow his government. The Lord will just chuckle at their ploys.[51]

When the seventh trumpet sounded, John heard the sound of worship and hymns. God responded to the worship by opening the sanctuary in heaven, accompanied by signs of his power.

His presence is open to us today because of the redeeming work of Jesus. When we worship, we enter his presence with sacrifices of praise and with thankful hearts.[52]

---

[51] Psalms 2:1–4.
[52] Psalms 100:4.

At the Mall

Read 2 Peter 3:3–10.

> And the rest of mankind, who were not killed by these plagues, did not repent of the works of their hands, so as not to worship demons, and the idols of gold and of silver and of brass and of stone and of wood, which can neither see nor hear nor walk; and they did not repent of their murders nor of their sorceries nor of their immorality nor of their thefts.
>
> Revelation 9:20–21 (NASB)

The shopping mall is a popular place. The windows have all the things "to make life complete": role-playing games like Dungeons and Dragons, 14 karat gold, silver and turquoise, solid brass, elegant porcelain, and solid oak. Angry horns are blasting in the parking lot. The gift store has zodiac key chains and coffee mugs. Outside the store, boys leer at the girls. The security guard just caught a shoplifter. The mall is a popular place. John described it in these verses.

Peter explained that people would rather ignore the gospel than turn away from their selfish lifestyles. God wants everyone to repent from sin, and he is willing to wait a while. But time will suddenly run out. God is offering forgiveness, life, and true happiness. He works from the inside out. Jesus will make life complete, if one will let him.

> PRAYER: Dear God, I want to turn away from all the sin and idols in my life. Please forgive me and come into my life. Amen.

FOR PERSONAL STUDY
The Seventh Trumpet   (11:14–19)

1. Why is the Lord being praised in verse 17?

2. List the events mentioned in verse 18.

3. What kind of feeling does the scene convey overall?

Review

Creation is groaning. The environment is being destroyed. The poor are getting poorer. It's not safe to walk the streets at night. But God has a plan.

In chapters 4 through 11 of Revelation, John tells us he saw the throne of God and a scroll which was sealed with seven seals. Throughout the Scriptures, the number seven is used to represent things that are complete. The scroll was completely sealed. Only Jesus was qualified to break open the seals and unroll the scroll. As He did, John saw a vision corresponding to each seal.

The seventh seal was special. When it was opened, seven angels were each given a trumpet. As the angels sounded their trumpets, John saw seven more visions. The scroll was completely revealed.

To apply it to our lives, consider the seven-sealed scroll as a panorama of our world. Look for parallels between our world and the visions John saw, and see how God's Word applies to us today. Let us first review the seven trumpets and summarize the meaning of the last seal, and then summarize all seven seals.

A bugle must be heard distinctly so that an army can prepare for battle.[53] God used seven bugle calls when the seventh seal was opened so that we can be completely prepared. The key to interpreting the seven bugle calls is found in 9:20–21.

> The rest of the people, who were not killed by these plagues, did not repent of the works of their hands to stop worshiping demons and idols of gold, silver, bronze, stone, and wood, which are not able to see, hear, or walk. And they did not repent of their murders, their sorceries, their sexual immorality, or their thefts.
> Revelation 9:20–21 (HCSB)

Mankind would not repent, even after six disasters. They could have repented, but they didn't. These verses imply that the message of the trumpets was "Repent!" Just like Moses before Pharaoh and just like Elijah before Israel, the message to our world is "Repent!" God does not want anyone to die; he wants everyone to respond to his bugle calls and repent.[54]

---
[53] 1 Corinthians 14:8.
[54] 2 Peter 3:9.

> Or do you despise the riches of His kindness, restraint, and patience, not recognizing that God's kindness is intended to lead you to repentance? But because of your hardness and unrepentant heart you are storing up wrath for yourself in the day of wrath, when God's righteous judgment is revealed. He will repay each one according to his works.
>
> Romans 2:4–6 (HCSB)

We can apply the seven bugle calls to our time. Local natural disasters like those of the first six trumpets are intended to get our attention. For example,

1. Forests fires

2. Seas polluted by red tide (toxic algae blooms)

3. Rivers poisoned by toxic chemicals and bacteria

4. Air filled with smog and volcanic ash clouds

5. Demonic torment

6. Deaths from volcanic eruptions

7. The second coming of Jesus

Creation's groans are telling the world to repent. When people experience natural disasters like the first six trumpets, some will realize that life is too fragile to manage alone. A disaster pushes them to repent and turn toward the Lord. Others are oblivious to the danger and just continue to live their ungodly lifestyles.

God has given us seven good reasons to repent. The seventh is the most important. Jesus will reign in righteousness. To most of the world, the second coming of Jesus is a threat. To us who believe, it is a promise. His coming is the best reason to repent now.

Now that we know the message of the seven bugle calls, which make up the seventh seal, let us consider the other seals and summarize the overall message of the seven-sealed scroll. The key to interpreting the seven-sealed scroll is found in 6:15–17.

> Then the kings of the earth, the nobles, the military commanders, the rich, the powerful, and every slave and free person hid in the caves and among the rocks of the mountains. And they said to the mountains and to the rocks, "Fall on us and hide us from the face of the One seated on the throne and from the wrath of the Lamb, because the great day of Their wrath has come! And who is able to stand?"
>
> Revelation 6:15–17 (HCSB)

The important people of the world, as well as ordinary folks, knew what the scroll meant. They recognized that God is righteous, that he has a right to be angry with the world, and that the time of reckoning has come. Instead of repenting, they called on the rocks to hide them from God's anger.

> For God's wrath is revealed from heaven against all godlessness and unrighteousness of people who by their unrighteousness suppress the truth, since what can be known about God is evident among them, because God has shown it to them.
> Romans 1:18–19 (HCSB)

We can apply the seven-sealed scroll to our time. Each of the first six scenes are familiar. They show us the effects of sin. The seventh seal reveals God's solution.

1. Oppression

2. War

3. Famine

4. Death from plagues

5. Martyrs

6. Catastrophes

7. God's message — Repent!

All the earth groans under the weight of sin. Creation, Christians, and the world's people feel its effects—death. Each of the first six seals reveals an aspect of that death. The seventh seal offers hope. "The free gift of God is eternal life in Christ Jesus our Lord."[55] To escape death, the world must repent.

> For we know that the whole creation has been groaning together with labor pains until now. And not only that, but we ourselves who have the Spirit as the firstfruits—we also groan within ourselves, eagerly waiting for adoption, the redemption of our bodies.
> Romans 8:22–23 (HCSB)

God cares for each of us personally. Even though all of creation is hurting from the results of sin, he understands my hurts and disappointments today, too. He is our hope, because we are eagerly waiting for Jesus to return. This hurting world will then be set free from the curse of sin, and we will live with him forever.

---

[55] Romans 6:23 (NASB).

FOR PERSONAL STUDY
Review—A Scroll with Seven Seals (4:1–11:19)

1. Review what the passage literally says about the seven trumpets. What do some of them have in common? (8:7–9:21 and 11:14–19)
2. What was the reaction of mankind to the first six trumpets? (9:20–21)
3. What is the theme of the seven trumpets?
4. Review the main idea of each of the first six seals. (6:1–17)
5. What was the reaction of mankind to the first six seals? (6:16–17)
6. What is the theme of the seven seals? (Remember, the seven trumpets as a whole are the vision of the seventh seal.)
7. How does each seal contribute to the picture?
8. What is the main idea of chapters 4 and 5?
9. How do the scenes of chapters 4 and 5 contribute to the message of the seven seals?
10. What connections do you see between the interlude in 10:1–11:13 and the main idea of the seven trumpets?
11. What connections do you seen between the interlude in 7:1–17 and the main idea of the seven seals?
12. What do chapters 4 through 11 teach us about the way God cares for his people?
13. What do chapters 4 through 11 teach us about the way God deals with mankind?

A Roaring Lion

Read 1 Peter 5:6–11.

> And the great dragon was thrown down, the serpent of old who is called the devil and Satan, who deceives the whole world; he was thrown down to the earth, and his angels were thrown down with him.
>
> Revelation 12:9 (NASB)

It's midnight in the jungle. No one can see anything in the darkness, unless he has cat-eyes. The roar of the lion can be heard five miles away. He wants everyone in his territory to know he is on the prowl. All competitors are intimidated.

The devil wants us to feel intimidated when he is on the prowl. He is hungry to victimize those God loves. Jesus, the Risen One, is more powerful than Satan or any of his demons, and he has given his authority to us. When confronted by the devil's roar, I must resist and stand firm. The Lord will give victory to his beloved.

PRAYER: Dear God, I trust you instead of worrying. I will resist the devil and be firm in my faith. Amen.

4

War

> "Okay, this will be by a secret ballot," he said, handing the slips of paper to two quickly appointed ushers who passed them out. "Let's just keep it simple. If you want to keep the pastor, say yes, and if you want to find someone else, say no." ...
>
> Writing a simple yes or no didn't take long, so almost immediately the ushers were passing the offering plates among the people.
>
> Guilo stood still in his corner, glaring at as many demons as would look at him. Some of the smaller, harassing spirits flitted about the sanctuary trying to see what people were marking on their ballots, and grinning, scowling, cheering, or cursing accordingly...
>
> After a bit of nervous chuckling John Coleman was selected by the yeas and Gordon Mayer by the nays to count the ballots. The two men took the offering plates full of ballots to the back pew. A flock of flapping, hissing demons converged on the scene, wanting to see the outcome.[1]

Frank Peretti's novel vividly dramatizes spiritual warfare that is behind the scenes of everyday life.

Spiritual warfare is not heroes with white hats conquering the forces of evil wearing black hats. It more often happens in the ordinary affairs of daily life, such as the church business meeting Frank Peretti described. Demons may flap, hiss, harass, and tempt, but people cast the votes and determine the outcome. We are at war.

Satan and his spiritual forces have declared war against God's people. Satan will try any tactic to make the gospel ineffective, but God has equipped us with just the right armor and weapons. The forces for evil may seem overwhelming, but God's power is greater.

---

[1] Frank E. Peretti, *This Present Darkness* (Westchester, Illinois: Crossway, 1986), p. 102. A novel portraying spiritual warfare, including characters who are angels and demons.

> Finally, be strengthened by the Lord and by His vast strength. Put on the full armor of God so that you can stand against the tactics of the Devil. For our battle is not against flesh and blood, but against the rulers, against the authorities, against the world powers of this darkness, against the spiritual forces of evil in the heavens. This is why you must take up the full armor of God, so that you may be able to resist in the evil day, and having prepared everything, to take your stand.
>
> Ephesians 6:10–13 (HCSB)

To be effective in battle, one must have the right equipment for both defense and attack. This passage in Ephesians goes on to list the spiritual qualities that comprise the armor of God, including the sword of the Spirit, the word of God.[2]

When overwhelmed in battle, one must call for reinforcements. We have no choice but to call on God to fight with us against Satan's spiritual forces.

To fight effectively, it is important to "know your enemy." If we assume that our opposition is simply circumstances, other people, or our own inadequacies, our efforts will be frustrated, because we do not know the real enemy, Satan and his spiritual forces. What does Revelation have to say about Satan's schemes, his strategy, and his tactics?

In chapters 12 through 16 of Revelation we discover who is involved in this spiritual war, what the strategies and tactics are, what our weapons are, and what the outcome will be.

"And a great sign appeared in heaven"[3] introduces the next series of visions. The signs are not explicitly numbered, as the seven seals were, but in each case, John saw something new in a new setting.

As shown in the following outline, chapter 12 through the first part of chapter 14 describes the first six signs. But before we read about the seventh sign, the remainder of chapter 14 is an interlude. The seventh sign was itself made up of seven parts. Chapter 15 introduces the seven bowls of God's wrath, and chapter 16 describes what happened as each was poured out. After the sixth bowl, there was an interlude, and then the seventh bowl was poured out, completing the picture of God's wrath.

III. Seven Signs

    1. The Dragon   12:1–17
    2. Beasts   12:18–13:18
    3. A New Song   14:1–5
    4. 1st Angel   The Gospel   14:6–7
    5. 2nd Angel   Babylon's Doom   14:8
    6. 3rd Angel   Marked   14:9–13

---

[2] Ephesians 6:17.
[3] 12:1 (NASB).

War

Illustration 4.1: A Woman and the Dragon   (12:1–17)

Interlude	Reapings	14:14–20
7. Seven Bowls		
Introduction	Songs	15:1–8
1st Bowl	Sores	16:1–2
2nd Bowl	Sea	16:3
3rd Bowl	Rivers and Springs	16:4–7
4th Bowl	Sun	16:8–9
5th Bowl	Darkness	16:10–11
6th Bowl	The Euphrates	16:12
Interlude	Three frogs	16:13–16
7th Bowl	Finished	16:17–21

War in Heaven

A woman. On a cloudless night, the stars seem to come alive with figures of animals, men, and women. The ancients saw special significance in the constellations. For example, when the magi saw the Messiah's star, they set out across the desert to pay homage to the Christ child.[4]

John too saw a sign in the sky. Read the first six verses of chapter 12.

Revelation 12:1–6 (HCSB)

> 1 A great sign appeared in heaven: a woman clothed with the sun, with the moon under her feet and a crown of 12 stars on her head. 2 She was pregnant and cried out in labor and agony as she was about to give birth. 3 Then another sign appeared in heaven: There was a great fiery red dragon having seven heads and 10 horns, and on his heads were seven diadems. 4 His tail swept away a third of the stars in heaven and hurled them to the earth. And the dragon stood in front of the woman who was about to give birth, so that when she did give birth he might devour her child. 5 But she gave birth to a Son—a male who is going to shepherd all nations with an iron scepter—and her child was caught up to God and to His throne. 6 The woman fled into the wilderness, where she had a place prepared by God, to be fed there for 1,260 days.

When John looked up, he saw a sign in the sky that looked like a pregnant woman. The moon was under her feet, stars were on her head, and in between

---

[4] Matthew 2:2.

she was "clothed with the sun." He saw another sign in the shape of a dragon positioned in front of the woman.

These images may have started as constellations, but the characters came alive in a spiritual drama. The woman gave birth to a son whom the dragon tried to kill. The dragon was so angry at his failure that he persecuted the woman and her children.

Let us first interpret her son. The child is identified as he "who was to rule all nations with a rod of iron."[5] This is a reference to Psalms 2:9 which indicates that the Messiah will rule the nations of the world with an iron scepter. Jesus quoted this same Psalm in his promise to Thyatira.[6] Thus, the child represents the Messiah. This is further supported by parallels in the life of Jesus with other details of the story. For example, Satan indeed wants to destroy him. Herod tried to kill him in Bethlehem. He indeed ascended to heaven after the resurrection.

Having identified the child, it is easier to identify the woman. A literal interpretation, Mary, the mother of Jesus, doesn't fit with other scriptures about Mary. Let's look for a broader meaning. The description of the woman is similar to this description of the Bride in Song of Songs.

> Who is this that appears like the dawn, fair as the moon, bright as the sun, majestic as the stars in procession?
>
> Song of Songs 6:10 (NIV)

The Bridegroom in Song of Songs obviously thinks his Bride is very beautiful. Similarly, the woman in John's vision was beautiful.

Isaiah portrayed Jerusalem as a woman giving birth to a nation, after years of desolation.[7] The woman of John's vision may represent the nation of Israel in history.

> Before Zion was in labor, she gave birth; before she was in pain, she delivered a boy.
>
> Isaiah 66:7 (HCSB)

After giving birth, the woman ran away from the dragon into the wilderness, where God took care of her. There is more about this later.

Verse 9 clearly identifies the dragon as Satan, and describes several aspects of his character: tempter, accuser, and deceiver. The serpent tempted Eve in the garden of Eden and deceived her.[8] Ever since, Satan has continued deceiving the whole world. The Greek word for *devil* in this passage means accuser, and the Hebrew word *Satan*[9] also means accuser or adversary. For example, Satan accused Job before God which led to the testing of Job's faith.[10]

---

[5]12:5 (KJV).
[6]2:27.
[7]Isaiah 66:7–13.
[8]Genesis 3:1–13.
[9]The Hebrew word *Satan* (*Strong's* No. 7854) was simply transliterated in the Greek New Testament. (The Greek word *Satan* (*Strong's* No. 4567).) The Greek word *diabolos* (*Strong's* No. 1228) is translated devil.
[10]Job 1:8–10.

Illustration 4.2: War in Heaven (12:7–12)

Paul admonished the church in Corinth[11] to be on guard against deception by Satan and his forces. We also should avoid being distracted from our relationship with Jesus. He may be clever at tempting, accusing, and deceiving, but it won't work on us. Jesus is interceding for us, justifying us before God and giving us the power to stand firm.

> Who can bring an accusation against God's elect? God is the One who justifies. Who is the one who condemns? Christ Jesus is the One who died, but even more, has been raised; He also is at the right hand of God and intercedes for us.
>
> Romans 8:33–34 (HCSB)

The dragon was red with seven heads and ten horns. Chapter 13 introduces a beast resembling the dragon. The heads and horns of the beast are explained in chapter 17.[12]

Some commentators interpret the stars swept from heaven as representing the angels which Satan took with him when he rebelled against God in the beginning.[13] These constituted his army mentioned in the following verses.

War in heaven. Read the next six verses of chapter 12.

Revelation 12:7–12 (HCSB)

> 7 Then war broke out in heaven: Michael and his angels fought against the dragon. The dragon and his angels also fought, 8 but he could not prevail, and there was no place for them in heaven any longer. 9 So the great dragon was thrown out—the ancient serpent, who is called the Devil and Satan, the one who deceives the whole world. He was thrown to earth, and his angels with him.
>
>   10 Then I heard a loud voice in heaven say:
>
>> The salvation and the power
>> and the kingdom of our God
>> and the authority of His Messiah
>> have now come,
>> because the accuser of our brothers
>> has been thrown out:
>> the one who accuses them
>> before our God day and night.
>> 11 They conquered him
>> by the blood of the Lamb
>> and by the word of their testimony,
>> for they did not love their lives
>> in the face of death.

---

[11] 2 Corinthians 11:3.
[12] 17:9 and 17:12.
[13] Isaiah 14:12–15.

> 12 Therefore rejoice, you heavens,
> and you who dwell in them!
> Woe to the earth and the sea,
> for the Devil has come down to you
> with great fury,
> because he knows he has a short time.

War in heaven raged between God's army of angels, led by Michael, and Satan with his army of angels. Michael is mentioned several time in the Scriptures, as an archangel, and as a prince.[14] In each case, he is engaged in angelic warfare. Satan lost the battle and was thrown out of heaven. Similarly, when Jesus' disciples were casting Satan's demons out of people, Jesus saw Satan's fall.[15] When Satan was thrown out, everyone in heaven rejoiced.

When we resist temptation, counter accusation, and hold to the truth, Satan is defeated in daily life. We too, can rejoice for these same reasons. The kingdom of God has arrived. Jesus has all authority and power. Salvation is available to us. All this is possible because Satan has been thrown out of heaven.[16] God doesn't have to listen to him anymore.

Satan tried to accuse the Christians, but they overcame him three ways: by the blood of Jesus, by telling others about him, and by dedicating themselves to him, even though it meant risking their lives.

I'm sure the angels in heaven were glad he was gone. But it wasn't going to be easy for those of us still on this Earth. Because Satan knew he would lose the war soon, he wanted to hurt God as much as he could by persecuting those God loves.

War on Earth. Read the remainder of chapter 12 of Revelation.

Revelation 12:13–17 (HCSB)

> 13 When the dragon saw that he had been thrown to earth, he persecuted the woman who gave birth to the male child. 14 The woman was given two wings of a great eagle, so that she could fly from the serpent's presence to her place in the wilderness, where she was fed for a time, times, and half a time. 15 From his mouth the serpent spewed water like a river flowing after the woman, to sweep her away in a torrent. 16 But the earth helped the woman. The earth opened its mouth and swallowed up the river that the dragon had spewed from his mouth. 17 So the dragon was furious with the woman and left to wage war against the rest of her offspring—those who keep God's commands and have the testimony about Jesus.

---

[14] Jude 1:9, Daniel 10:13,21, and Daniel 12:1.
[15] Luke 10:17–18.
[16] 12:10.

The dragon's first target in this vision was the woman who gave birth to the Messiah. In verse 6, it says the woman fled into the wilderness. In verse 14, it explains how she got there. God provided an eagle for the woman's escape. This is similar to imagery describing the exodus from Egypt.

> You have seen what I did to the Egyptians and how I carried you on eagles' wings and brought you to Me.
>
> Exodus 19:4 (HCSB)

Even though the wilderness is a barren place, God provided for her there. Similarly, God provided manna for Moses and the children of Israel. God wants to provide for us as well at those times in life that seem barren.

The woman was in the desert about three and one half years (1,260 days is 42 months times 30 days per month). This time period reminds us of the three and one half years of drought in the days of Elijah.[17] During that time, God miraculously provided food and water for Elijah. This association reinforces the principle of God's provision for us.

After a while, Satan caught up with her and tried to sweep her away with a flood, but she was protected. This reminds one of God's protection for the Jewish people over the centuries.

The devil must have been pretty frustrated. Having failed to sweep away the woman, he looked for somebody else to persecute. He went after those who keep the commands of God and have the testimony of Jesus, namely, the Christians.

Therefore, it's not surprising that we face attacks from Satan and his forces. The battle lines have been drawn between God's forces and Satan's. Satan has been at war with God's forces since time began, but Satan has been defeated in heaven, and he soon will be defeated on Earth.

Whether we like it or not, the church is engaged in a spiritual war. Who is our enemy? What are his tactics? What are our weapons? What is our strategy? Revelation helps us answer these questions, and reminds us who will win in the end.

FOR PERSONAL STUDY
The Dragon   (12:1–17)

1. Read Revelation 19:5 and Psalms 2:9. Who is the child?

2. Who is the dragon?

3. Rephrase the announcement in verses 10–12 in you own words.

4. Why did the dragon persecute the woman? (verses 13–17)

5. What is God's goal in this scene?

6. What does this passage teach us to expect from Satan?

---

[17]James 5:17, 1 Kings 17:1, and Luke 4:25.

Illustration 4.3: Beasts   (12:18–14:20)

Big Brother

> The poster with the enormous face gazed from the wall. It was one of those pictures which are so contrived that the eyes follow you about when you move. BIG BROTHER IS WATCHING YOU, the caption beneath it ran.[18]

In *1984: A Novel*, George Orwell described a world where the State controlled every aspect of life. The Ministry of Truth twisted language. The Thought Police could monitor one's every word and move. A slip of the tongue could have brutal consequences.

The Beast. In the dragon's domain, a slip could likewise have brutal consequences. Read 12:18 through the first ten verses of chapter 13.[19]

Revelation 12:18–13:10 (HCSB)

---

18 He stood on the sand of the sea.

1 And I saw a beast coming up out of the sea. He had 10 horns and seven heads. On his horns were 10 diadems, and on his heads were blasphemous names. 2 The beast I saw was like a leopard, his feet were like a bear's, and his mouth was like a lion's mouth. The dragon gave him his power, his throne, and great authority. 3 One of his heads appeared to be fatally wounded, but his fatal wound was healed. The whole earth was amazed and followed the beast. 4 They worshiped the dragon because he gave authority to the beast. And they worshiped the beast, saying, "Who is like the beast? Who is able to wage war against him?"

5 A mouth was given to him to speak boasts and blasphemies. He was also given authority to act for 42 months. 6 He began to speak blasphemies against God: to blaspheme His name and His dwelling—those who dwell in heaven. 7 And he was permitted to wage war against the saints and to conquer them. He was also given authority over every tribe, people, language, and nation. 8 All those who live on the earth will worship him, everyone whose name was not written from the foundation of the world in the book of life of the Lamb who was slaughtered.

9 If anyone has an ear, he should listen:

10 If anyone is destined for captivity,
into captivity he goes.
If anyone is to be killed with a sword,
with a sword he will be killed.

This demands the perseverance and faith of the saints.

---

[18] George Orwell, *1984: A Novel* (New York: Penguin, 1981), p. 5.
[19] Some translations put 12:18 either in 12:17 or 13:1.

A beast emerged from the sea. This creature bore a striking resemblance to the dragon. They both had seven heads, ten horns, and crowns. Blasphemous names on the beast's heads made it clear whose side he was on.

The dragon's crowns were on his heads, symbols of authority. The beast's crowns were on his horns. The horns of an angry bull are his instruments of power. The authority of the beast was based on power.

> Again, I observed all the acts of oppression being done under the sun. Look at the tears of those who are oppressed; they have no one to comfort them. Power is with those who oppress them; they have no one to comfort them.
>
> Ecclesiastes 4:1 (HCSB)

The power of the State (the government) is often similar to this beast. In ancient times, an all-powerful king embodied the government of a nation. For more than two centuries now, nation-states, in the form of republics, constitutional monarchies, and military dictatorships, have dominated the world scene instead of autocratic kings. Recent history is full of examples of nation-states that have oppressed their neighbors, their own people, and Christians, in particular. When "might makes right," many are oppressed and suffer. When considering our own nation, we must be careful to not let patriotism or partisan loyalty blind us to abuse of power by the government.

This one beast had characteristics of a leopard, a bear, and a lion, and also had the authority of Satan. Similarly, Daniel had a vision of four beasts like a lion, a bear, a leopard, and a dreadful, terrifying beast.[20] Just as God judged the beasts in Daniel's vision, He will judge this beast, too.

The beast had a head which looked like it had been killed, but the wound was amazingly healed. The world's people were so impressed that they worshiped him. They thought he was omnipotent. In his arrogance, he blasphemed God and all he stands for. This represents a counterfeit of the resurrection of Jesus, and a counterfeit of God's omnipotence.

The beast was allowed to overcome Christians, and to take over the whole world for a while. Everyone on Earth worshiped him, except those whose names have been "written from the foundation of the world in the book of life of the Lamb who was slaughtered."[21] In other words, believers in Jesus seemed to lose the war, but still did not worship him. When naked power seems to take over, a believer remains true to Jesus.

After describing the beast, John said, "If any man have an ear, let him hear."[22] Apparently, John thought the interpretation of the beast was obvious. In any era, Satan's agents of oppression are not hard to find. Oppression, jail, executions, and war will continue, but irrespective of the threat of captivity or death, Christians must persevere.

---

[20] Daniel 7:3–12.
[21] 13:8 (HCSB).
[22] 13:9 (KJV).

The False Prophet. Read the remainder of chapter 13 of Revelation.

Revelation 13:11–18 (HCSB)

> 11 Then I saw another beast coming up out of the earth; he had two horns like a lamb, but he sounded like a dragon. 12 He exercises all the authority of the first beast on his behalf and compels the earth and those who live on it to worship the first beast, whose fatal wound was healed. 13 He also performs great signs, even causing fire to come down from heaven to earth in front of people. 14 He deceives those who live on the earth because of the signs that he is permitted to perform on behalf of the beast, telling those who live on the earth to make an image of the beast who had the sword wound and yet lived. 15 He was permitted to give a spirit to the image of the beast, so that the image of the beast could both speak and cause whoever would not worship the image of the beast to be killed. 16 And he requires everyone—small and great, rich and poor, free and slave—to be given a mark on his right hand or on his forehead, 17 so that no one can buy or sell unless he has the mark: the beast's name or the number of his name.
>
> 18 Here is wisdom: The one who has understanding must calculate the number of the beast, because it is the number of a man. His number is 666.

Verse 11 introduces another beast which came out of the land, rather than the sea. For convenience, we will continue to call the beast from the sea the *Beast*, and we will call the beast from the land the *False Prophet*, as in Revelation 19:20. The False Prophet looked like a lamb, but spoke like Satan. Just as the Beast tried to counterfeit the resurrection power of Jesus, the False Prophet was trying to counterfeit the Lamb of God. Jesus said "My sheep hear my voice."[23] If we continue to listen to the voice of Jesus, namely, the Holy Spirit in our hearts, we will not be fooled by anyone who tries to equate true religion with worship of worldly power.

The False Prophet and the Beast worked together. The False Prophet's job was to convince the world's people to worship the Beast. He did this with signs and wonders, even fire from heaven.

One of his tactics was to make a statue of the Beast for people to worship. To make the Beast seem more divine, he made the idol appear to come alive. The False Prophet had authority to execute those who would not worship the idol of the Beast.

Nebuchadnezzar tried that too. He built a large idol, and required all the government officials to worship it, including Shadrach, Meshach, and Abednego, who were Israelites in exile. When they refused to worship the idol,

---

[23] John 10:27 (KJV).

Nebuchadnezzar tried to execute them in the fiery furnace. It didn't work; Shadrach, Meshach, and Abednego came through the furnace unscathed.[24]

We applied the picture of the Beast to the power of the State. We can apply the False Prophet to establishment religion, mainstream news media, or any institution, which fosters patriotism or party loyalty to such a degree that it is worship of the State.

John's vision does not tell us what happened to the False Prophet's statue of the Beast, but Nebuchadnezzar had a dream of a great image which represented the kingdoms of Earth. It was crushed by a stone from God, which represented the Messiah's kingdom.[25] I suspect the same thing will happen to the statue of the Beast.

Another of the False Prophet's tactics was to control the economy, so that only those loyal to the Beast could buy and sell. To document one's allegiance, one had to have the mark of the Beast. In chapter 7, God's servants were marked by his signet. Similarly, we are marked for God by the Holy Spirit who lives in us. We belong to him. The mark of the Beast represents a counterfeit to the seal of the Holy Spirit in our lives.

It seems that our times are preoccupied with economics. Every news event is analyzed in dollars and cents. Materialism is perhaps the most widespread religion in the world. Paul explains that greed is the same as idolatry, and is just as bad as sexual immorality.[26] The love of money is the source of many other evils as well,[27] so we shouldn't be surprised that Satan exploits materialism.

Without realizing it, many Christians have the same materialistic values as everyone else. This makes some believers vulnerable to economic control by the enemy. Repentance is called for when materialism creeps in. Would one rather have a credit card, or the Holy Spirit?

John gives a clue to the interpretation of the Beast. His "number" is 666. In ancient times, a person's number was calculated by adding up the letters of his name, where each letter had a number associated with it: one for A; two for B; and so on. John must have thought the identity of the beast was obvious, but Bible scholars have debated the meaning of 666 ever since. Each generation seems to think that the most evil political leader of their day is the Beast.

In each generation, Satan has his agents of power and deception at work in the world. We can apply the sign of the Beast and False Prophet to local people and institutions, but they are only temporary participants in the real war in the spiritual realm.

> For our battle is not against flesh and blood, but against the rulers, against the authorities, against the world powers of this darkness, against the spiritual forces of evil in the heavens.
>
> Ephesians 6:12 (HCSB)

---

[24] Daniel 3:1–30.
[25] Daniel 2:31–44.
[26] Ephesians 5:5.
[27] 1 Timothy 6:10.

FOR PERSONAL STUDY
Beasts (12:18–13:18)

1. What was the relationship between the dragon and the Beast?

2. What did the people of the world think about the Beast?

3. What was the relationship between the beast from the sea (the Beast) and the beast from the land (the False Prophet)?

4. How did the False Prophet contribute to Satan's plan?

5. What should God's people to expect from Satan's representatives?

6. What forces in your life are like the Beast and the False Prophet? How are they similar? How are they different?

A New Song

As the music played, the soloist sang with her hands. The deaf in the congregation recognized that it was Sign Language. The rest of us saw a beautiful enactment of the song. This was not just for the deaf. The motion conveyed overflowing joy to us all in a new way.

God's faithful ones had a new song as well. Read this section's Scripture passage.

Revelation 14:1–5 (HCSB)

---

1 Then I looked, and there on Mount Zion stood the Lamb, and with Him were 144,000 who had His name and His Father's name written on their foreheads. 2 I heard a sound from heaven like the sound of cascading waters and like the rumbling of loud thunder. The sound I heard was also like harpists playing on their harps. 3 They sang a new song before the throne and before the four living creatures and the elders, but no one could learn the song except the 144,000 who had been redeemed from the earth. 4 These are the ones not defiled with women, for they have kept their virginity. These are the ones who follow the Lamb wherever He goes. They were redeemed from the human race as the firstfruits for God and the Lamb. 5 No lie was found in their mouths; they are blameless.

The next sign was the Lamb and 144 thousand saints standing on Mount Zion. We know the 144 thousand belong to Jesus. Rather than the mark of the Beast, a counterfeit, they had God's seal.[28] Because they belonged to Jesus, they were protected from God's judgment of mankind.[29]

---

[28] 7:3–8 and 13:16–17.
[29] 9:4.

A sound from heaven like harps accompanied their song. It was loud, worshipful, and fresh. Because they were purchased by the blood of Jesus, their song was overflowing with joy.

> And the redeemed of the Lord will return and come to Zion with singing, crowned with unending joy. Joy and gladness will overtake them, and sorrow and sighing will flee.
> Isaiah 35:10 (HCSB)

They sang a new song, which only they could learn.[30] New songs can be accompanied with instrumental music and dance.[31] Musical improvisation unto the Lord is an example of a new song which flows from heart. It is not learned by rote, and cannot be repeated.

In some churches, spontaneous celebration, much like folk dancing, expresses feelings of worship, like David did before the ark of the Lord.[32] In other churches, prepared interpretive dance expresses the worshipful meditation of the choreographer and dancers.

In chapter 7, we saw that the 144 thousand were all servants of God. We can identify with them. The 144 thousand were undefiled. They were pure, waiting for their marriage to the Lamb.[33] The 144 thousand followed the Lamb. Like sheep following a shepherd, we should follow Jesus wherever He leads us. To do this, we must each listen to the Holy Spirit inside.[34] The 144 thousand were first fruits to God. The Old Testament Law required an offering to the Lord of the first crops to ripen, "first fruits."[35] We, who are born-again, are like an offering of first fruits from Jesus to the Father.[36] The 144 thousand were not liars. Their zeal for truth stood in stark contrast to the deception of Satan's forces.

God has an answer to the False Prophet's tactics. Instead of a mark, God gives us the Holy Spirit. Instead of a statue that talks, he gives us a new song. Instead of following the Beast, we follow Jesus.

Not only should we imitate the godly character of the 144 thousand, but we can also imitate their unrestrained worship. Unrestrained worship is a weapon of spiritual warfare.

> Hallelujah! Sing to the Lord a new song, His praise in the assembly of the godly. Let Israel celebrate its Maker; let the children of Zion rejoice in their King. Let them praise His name with dancing and make music to Him with tambourine and lyre. For Yahweh takes pleasure in His people; He adorns the humble with salvation.
> Psalms 149:1–4 (HCSB)

---

[30] A new song can be a means of evangelism. Psalms 40:1–3.
[31] Psalms 33:1–5 and Psalms 149:1–4.
[32] 2 Samuel 6:14–15.
[33] 19:5-10.
[34] John 10:27–28.
[35] Deuteronomy 18:4 and Proverbs 3:9–10.
[36] James 1:18.

Work that Lasts

Read Philippians 1:19–21.

"Blessed are the dead who die in the Lord from now on." "Yes," says the Spirit, "that they may rest from their labors, for their deeds follow with them."[a]

Revelation 14:13 (NASB)

The funeral had just finished. The music was uplifting, the message was comforting. As I turned to leave, I was shocked to see that so many had come.

Joan worked at a small manufacturing company for nine years. When business slowed down, she was laid off, and went to work someplace else. About two and a half years later, she died of cancer.

Even though two and a half years is a long time, the boss had closed the plant for the afternoon, and about fifty from the plant had come to the funeral. The soloist sang about the loving concern each of them had experienced from her. The minister told them once more about the love of Jesus, just like she would have.

She was the one who was always sympathetic when life's troubles seemed overwhelming. She was the one who could talk about Jesus in almost any conversation. I want my life to be more like Joan's. I want to share His love in words and actions like she did.

Now she can rest from her labors. Her love for those fellow employees follows her.

> PRAYER: Lord, make me an instrument of your love to all kinds of people, especially those at my job. Amen.

---

[a] Second beatitude of Revelation.

FOR PERSONAL STUDY
A New Song (14:1–5)

1. List the characteristics of the 144 thousand. Summarize these in one phrase.

2. Describe the relationship between the Lamb and the 144 thousand.

3. What are some examples of new songs that you have seen?

4. What aspects of your worship time are similar to the worship of the 144 thousand for the Lamb? How can you improve the quality of your own worship?

Three Weapons

Learning to use an M-16 rifle was probably the most important skill taught in my Army Basic Training. Day after day, we marched to the rifle range to practice. We shot at fixed targets and popups while standing, kneeling, and lying down until we could pass the test. In the infantry, using one's weapons well is a matter of life and death.

Using our spiritual weapons well may also be a matter of life and death. Read this section's Scripture passage.

Revelation 14:6–13 (HCSB)

> 6 Then I saw another angel flying high overhead, having the eternal gospel to announce to the inhabitants of the earth—to every nation, tribe, language, and people. 7 He spoke with a loud voice: "Fear God and give Him glory, because the hour of His judgment has come. Worship the Maker of heaven and earth, the sea and springs of water."
>
> 8 A second angel followed, saying: "It has fallen, Babylon the Great has fallen, who made all nations drink the wine of her sexual immorality, which brings wrath."
>
> 9 And a third angel followed them and spoke with a loud voice: "If anyone worships the beast and his image and receives a mark on his forehead or on his hand, 10 he will also drink the wine of God's wrath, which is mixed full strength in the cup of His anger. He will be tormented with fire and sulfur in the sight of the holy angels and in the sight of the Lamb, 11 and the smoke of their torment will go up forever and ever. There is no rest day or night for those who worship the beast and his image, or anyone who receives the mark of his name. 12 This demands the perseverance of the saints, who keep God's commands and their faith in Jesus."
>
> 13 Then I heard a voice from heaven saying, "Write: The dead who die in the Lord from now on are blessed."

> "Yes," says the Spirit, "let them rest from their labors, for their works follow them!"

This section consists of three signs describing spiritual weapons, followed by a beatitude.

The gospel. The next sign was an angel in midair with the gospel. He urged everyone to worship the Lord, because judgment has arrived. The Lord has the right to judge, because he is our creator.

The gospel is for everyone. Paul explained that the gospel is both for Jews and for gentiles.[37] It doesn't matter what your demographic category is. Faith in Jesus is what counts. Jesus said that when the gospel is preached to all kinds of people, his second coming will be near.[38]

All kinds of people can certainly hear the gospel today. Radio and TV broadcast the gospel into every neighborhood on Planet Earth. Jet airplanes, helicopters and four-wheel-drive vehicles take believers over every terrain. Bible translation based on modern linguistics is making the scriptures available in one language after another. The love of God penetrates walls of ethnic hostility. No family is exempt from the call of the gospel.

There is no time to procrastinate. Soon it will be too late to reverence, honor, and worship the Lord. He has a right to be angry at the godlessness, vice, and corruption that has marred his creation. No one can say, "I didn't know," because his power and nature are revealed by the heavens, the land, the sea, and springs of water.[39] The Great Commission[40] is an urgent task, because God's judgment is near. As the gospel is spread, people in Satan's grip are converted into allies. The gospel is a weapon of spiritual warfare.

Babylon is fallen. The next sign was another angel announcing, "Babylon is fallen." The details of John's vision of Babylon are in chapters 17 and 18, but at this point, let us consider what the Old Testament had to say about ancient Babylon. The Old Testament prophets frequently portrayed Israel as God's bride. Accordingly, Israel's worship of idols was called adultery. The prophets foretold that Babylon would conquer Israel because of her unfaithfulness.

Babylon may have been used by God to discipline Israel, but Babylon was by no means innocent. Babylon was the greatest city of its time. Its armies seemed invincible, its wealth immeasurable, and its gods innumerable. Isaiah prophesied, "Babylon has fallen, has fallen! All the images of its gods lie shattered on the ground!"[41] Jeremiah condemned Babylon's armies for merciless slaughter and cruelty.[42]

---

[37] Romans 1:16–17.
[38] Matthew 24:14.
[39] Romans 1:18–20.
[40] Matthew 28:18–20.
[41] Isaiah 21:9 (NIV).
[42] Jeremiah 51:47–49.

Babylon was a gold cup in the Lord's hand, making the whole earth drunk. The nations drank her wine; therefore, the nations go mad. Suddenly Babylon fell and was shattered. Wail for her; get balm for her wound—perhaps she can be healed.[43]

Jeremiah 51:7–8 (HCSB)

The image of drunkenness is also used in Revelation. The seductive idolatry of ancient Babylon continued into Roman times, and on into our own. The idols may have changed from gold images to paper money or Hollywood glamour, but the spiritual fornication is the same.

We live in a corrupt society, too. There are the obvious problems of violence, drug addiction, racism, abortion, pornography, bribery, and fraud, and the less obvious, such as materialism, greed, sexual immorality, and propaganda. The immorality of our times cannot be ignored.

At the rifle range, one has to see the target before shooting at it. Recognition of sin is a prerequisite to receiving the gospel. Proclaiming that "Babylon is fallen" is a weapon of spiritual warfare.

Mark of the Beast. The next sign was a third angel proclaiming what will happen to those receiving the mark of the Beast.

The Beast and the False Prophet thought they had the upper hand. They engineered a counterfeit resurrection, convincing people to worship the Beast. They killed anyone who would not worship the image of the Beast. They controlled the economy by requiring special identification. Most people went along.

We can apply this to confrontations between the world system and God's way. To go along with the world is the same as identifying with Satan's forces rather than with Christ. The third angel proclaimed that those who went along with the Beast and False Prophet will feel the full force of God's wrath. They will be tormented with unrelenting fire forever.

Knowing the end of the story was encouraging to the Christians. They did not yield to the tactics of the Beast and False Prophet. They were steadfast. They continued to be faithful to Jesus and to do what he said.

Even though the Beast and False Prophet killed some, believers are blessed anyway. They have rest from their labors, while the followers of the Beast have no rest from their torment. Steadfastness is a weapon of spiritual warfare.

Spiritual warfare takes place on a different battlefield than military warfare. The world tries to coerce with threats of violence, but loses the hearts and minds of the people. Spiritual weapons are able to change hearts and minds to be pleasing to God.

> For though we live in the world, we do not wage war as the world does. The weapons we fight with are not the weapons of the world. On the contrary, they have divine power to demolish strongholds. We demolish arguments and every pretension that sets itself up

---

[43]"Get balm for her wound—perhaps she can be healed," is said sarcastically.

against the knowledge of God, and we take captive every thought to make it obedient to Christ.

2 Corinthians 10:3–5 (NIV)

FOR PERSONAL STUDY
Three Angels   (14:6–13)

1. Read Jeremiah 25:14-29. What do you associate with the phrase *wine of wrath*?

2. What is the main event of each announcement?

3. What is the main idea of verses 12–13? How is this related to the announcements?

4. What is the message of the announcements taken together?

FOR PERSONAL STUDY
Armor   (Ephesians 6:10–20)

Read Ephesians 6:10–20. Chapters 12 and 13 of Revelation vividly portray the warfare between God's people and Satan's forces.

1. What weapons do Satan's forces use?

2. Describe the enemy in this passage in Ephesians:

    - Who is he?
    - What can he do against us?
    - What kind of tactics does he use?

3. List the pieces of the "whole armor of God."

4. Describe an everyday situation that illustrates the protection of each piece of armor.

5. How do we "put on" this armor?

6. What is the main idea of Ephesians 6:18–20? How are these verses related to the rest of the passage?

7. Pray for each person in your Bible study group and for other believers.

Harvests

The big combines were mowing great swaths across golden fields. Wheat harvest had arrived in Kansas. The wheat must be cut before the next summer shower spoils the crop. A combine is much too expensive for most farmers to own, so a farmer will hire a combine crew to harvest his wheat. The crew will work all summer from Texas to Canada as the wheat harvest progresses northward.

Jesus has recruited us to work in his harvest as it progresses from place to place. Read the remainder of chapter 14 of Revelation.

Revelation 14:14–20 (HCSB)

> 14 Then I looked, and there was a white cloud, and One like the Son of Man was seated on the cloud, with a gold crown on His head and a sharp sickle in His hand. 15 Another angel came out of the sanctuary, crying out in a loud voice to the One who was seated on the cloud, "Use your sickle and reap, for the time to reap has come, since the harvest of the earth is ripe." 16 So the One seated on the cloud swung His sickle over the earth, and the earth was harvested.
>
> 17 Then another angel who also had a sharp sickle came out of the sanctuary in heaven. 18 Yet another angel, who had authority over fire, came from the altar, and he called with a loud voice to the one who had the sharp sickle, "Use your sharp sickle and gather the clusters of grapes from earth's vineyard, because its grapes have ripened." 19 So the angel swung his sickle toward earth and gathered the grapes from earth's vineyard, and he threw them into the great winepress of God's wrath. 20 Then the press was trampled outside the city, and blood flowed out of the press up to the horses' bridles for about 180 miles.

This scene is an interlude between the sixth and seventh signs, just as we have had interludes before. In the first part, one like the "son of man" harvested grain. In the second part, an angel from God's presence harvested grapes.

Wheat. The one on the cloud looked like a "son of man." This is probably a reference to Jesus. He often referred to himself by this title. Jesus is the King of Kings, and he will return to earth in the clouds.

Jesus frequently used harvesting grain to illustrate the kingdom of God.[44] He made it clear that the grain is people who have responded to the gospel.[45] Jesus sent his disciples to sow by preaching the gospel, and to reap by making

---
[44] Mark 4:26–29.
[45] Matthew 9:35–38.

disciples. This kind of harvest began during Jesus' ministry and continues today.[46]

In the Parable of Wheat and Tares, Jesus applied harvest time to the end of the age, when he will come again. As in his other parables, the grain represents those who have received the gospel, "sons of the kingdom." Jesus interpreted this parable explicitly. "The harvest is the end of the age, and the harvesters are angels."[47] When he returns, the angels will gather believers from all over the world to be with him forever.[48] Revelation uses this same imagery. The grain is ripe. Jesus is supervising the harvest.

As we read these few verses in Revelation, we can meditate on our mission to make disciples. When Christ comes again, the opportunity for harvest will be over.

Grapes. The second part of this interlude is about another kind of harvest, a harvest of grapes. From ancient times, grapes in a vat have been tread to make grape juice for wine-making.

Since grape juice flowing from the winepress can look like blood on a battlefield, reaping and pressing of grapes was used in the Old Testament as a metaphor for the bloodshed of battle.[49] The same metaphor is used in John's vision. The angel harvested the grapes and threw them into a wine press, which, we are told, represents God's anger against sin. To give us an idea of how great the sin was, the blood from the wine press flowed out like a flood, up to a horse's bridle and outward for sixteen hundred *stadia* (about 180 miles).[50]

The interlude shows us two sides of spiritual warfare on a personal level: the harvest of believers for Jesus, and the harvest of God's wrath against sin. Each person must choose whether to follow Jesus, and thus choose a harvest.

FOR PERSONAL STUDY
Reapings   (14:14–20)

1. What characteristics of a harvest are emphasized in each reaping?

2. For each of the questions below, write an answer for the first reaping and for the second reaping. Compare your answers.

   Who did it?
   What was reaped?
   Where did orders come from?
   What was the outcome?
   What does it represent?

---

[46] John 4:35–38.
[47] Matthew 13:24–30,36–43 (HCSB).
[48] Matthew 24:31.
[49] For example, Joel 3:13–14 and Isaiah 63:2–4.
[50] A *stadion* was a Roman unit of length, equal to about 200 meters. Herbert Lockyer, ed., *Nelson's Illustrated Bible Dictionary* (Nashville: Thomas Nelson, 1986), s.v. *weights and measures*.

For Who He Is

Read Deuteronomy 32:1–4.

Who shall not fear You, O Lord, and glorify Your name? For You alone are holy. For all nations shall come and worship before You, For Your judgments have been manifested.
Revelation 15:4 (NKJV)

God deserves my worship. Not only do I praise him for what he has done for me, but I also worship him from the heart just for who he is.

Like the shelter of a huge rock in the desert, he is my Rock. There is safety in his presence. I can trust him when I feel afraid.

His craftsmanship is flawless. He is thorough and meticulous in everything he does. When my life is in his hands, I can trust him to take care of all the details.

He is just. He knows the truth already. He isn't fooled by excuses. He doesn't care about technicalities. He is never unfair, or biased. His justice is guaranteed.

He is faithful. He is always steady when I am having ups and downs. He will always do what he says he will do. He is the same yesterday, today, and forever.

He is righteous. He never condones sin. He is holy.

PRAYER: O Lord, I revere and glorify you, because you are holy. All the world will join in worshiping you, because your justice will be seen by everyone. Amen.

The Wrath of God

After six signs and an interlude, the seventh sign itself had seven parts, namely, seven bowls of plagues. This is similar to the seventh seal, which had seven parts, namely, seven trumpets. A scene in heaven introduced seven bowls, followed by scenes on Earth as each bowl of plagues was poured out. The following shows the outline of this section, covering chapters 15 and 16.

7th Sign	Seven Bowls	
Introduction	Songs	15:1–8
1st Bowl	Sores	16:1–2
2nd Bowl	Sea	16:3
3rd Bowl	Rivers and Springs	16:4–7
4th Bowl	Sun	16:8–9
5th Bowl	Darkness	16:10–11
6th Bowl	The Euphrates	16:12
Interlude	Three frogs	16:13–16
7th Bowl	Finished	16:17–21

Like the first sign, the seventh was a sign in heaven. God holds the high ground in this spiritual battle. The last weapon of spiritual warfare is God's wrath against sin.

The Choir

The choir of the little country church consisted of dedicated and enthusiastic volunteers. Everyone was welcome. They sang at least two specials each Sunday, plus solos, often on short notice. The music may not have been refined, but the gospel harmony was from the heart. In another church, great works of sacred music were performed each Sunday. A professor of music directed from the organ. To assure quality, the core of the choir had been hired. Volunteers were carefully selected after an audition. The music was beautiful, but it was just a performance.

God's choir is made of those who volunteer to persevere for Jesus. Read chapter 15 of Revelation.

> Revelation 15:1–8 (HCSB)
>
> 1 Then I saw another great and awe-inspiring sign in heaven: seven angels with the seven last plagues, for with them, God's wrath will be completed. 2 I also saw something like a sea of glass mixed with

fire, and those who had won the victory over the beast, his image, and the number of his name, were standing on the sea of glass with harps from God. 3 They sang the song of God's servant Moses and the song of the Lamb:

> Great and awe-inspiring are Your works,
> Lord God, the Almighty;
> righteous and true are Your ways,
> King of the Nations.
> 4 Lord, who will not fear
> and glorify Your name?
> Because You alone are holy,
> for all the nations will come
> and worship before You
> because Your righteous acts
> have been revealed.

5 After this I looked, and the heavenly sanctuary—the tabernacle of testimony—was opened. 6 Out of the sanctuary came the seven angels with the seven plagues, dressed in clean, bright linen, with gold sashes wrapped around their chests. 7 One of the four living creatures gave the seven angels seven gold bowls filled with the wrath of God who lives forever and ever. 8 Then the sanctuary was filled with smoke from God's glory and from His power, and no one could enter the sanctuary until the seven plagues of the seven angels were completed.

The scene is set in heaven on a sea of glass, before the throne of God in heaven.[51] The choir in heaven consisted of those who were victorious over the Beast and all his tactics. Their victory was won by perseverance, namely, by doing what God says, and by keeping their faith in Jesus.[52] I'd much rather be in that choir than with the Beast's crowd, who ended up in eternal torment.[53]

The choir was praising God for his justice and authority. He is not like mankind; he is holy. All that he does is amazing, so that all kinds of people want to worship him.

Many people focus on God's love for mankind so much, that they think he would never hurt anyone. This sign teaches that God indeed is angry. The plagues came from the presence of God in the heavenly Holy of Holies. In the Tabernacle built by Moses, the Holy of Holies was the innermost room. It was where God dwelled with Israel. A similar Tabernacle in heaven is pictured here. The innermost room is often translated *temple*.

The bowls with the wrath of God were given to the angels by one of the creatures at the throne of God. In chapter four, we saw that those creatures

---

[51] 4:6.
[52] 14:12.
[53] 14:9–10.

The Wrath of God 16:1–12

represented all of creation. This gives us a hint that the instrument for the plagues is creation.

Once angels with the plagues were on their way, the heavenly Holy of Holies filled with smoke, so that no one could come into God's presence until sin had been dealt with.

FOR PERSONAL STUDY
Songs   (15:1–8)

1. How is the scene in heaven related to the seven plagues?

2. What is the main idea of the hymn? (verses 3–4) Why are they praising God?

3. Sit quietly. Close your eyes. Praise God from your heart for the same reasons.

Plagues

> When the Lord saw that man's wickedness was widespread on the earth and that every scheme his mind thought of was nothing but evil all the time, the Lord regretted that He had made man on the earth, and He was grieved in His heart. Then the Lord said, "I will wipe off from the face of the earth mankind, whom I created, together with the animals, creatures that crawl, and birds of the sky—for I regret that I made them." Noah, however, found favor in the sight of the Lord.
>
> Genesis 6:5–8 (HCSB)

In Noah's time, mankind's wickedness had become so pervasive that God had to clean up the mess. The Flood was God's judgment against the sin of mankind. This natural disaster killed everyone except those with Noah in the ark. People and animals drowned. All the forests and fields were destroyed. Mankind's sin caused tremendous destruction in all of the land.

God has not changed. He still hates sin. Read this section's Scripture.

Revelation 16:1–12 (HCSB)

> 1 Then I heard a loud voice from the sanctuary saying to the seven angels, "Go and pour out the seven bowls of God's wrath on the earth." 2 The first went and poured out his bowl on the earth, and severely painful sores broke out on the people who had the mark of the beast and who worshiped his image.
>
> 3 The second poured out his bowl into the sea. It turned to blood like a dead man's, and all life in the sea died.
>
> 4 The third poured out his bowl into the rivers and the springs of water, and they became blood. 5 I heard the angel of the waters say:

> You are righteous,
> who is and who was, the Holy One,
> for You have decided these things.
> 6 Because they poured out
> the blood of the saints and the prophets,
> You also gave them blood to drink;
> they deserve it!
>
> 7 Then I heard someone from the altar say:
>
> Yes, Lord God, the Almighty,
> true and righteous are Your judgments.
>
> 8 The fourth poured out his bowl on the sun. He was given the power to burn people with fire, 9 and people were burned by the intense heat. So they blasphemed the name of God, who had the power over these plagues, and they did not repent and give Him glory.
> 10 The fifth poured out his bowl on the throne of the beast, and his kingdom was plunged into darkness. People gnawed their tongues because of their pain 11 and blasphemed the God of heaven because of their pains and their sores, yet they did not repent of their actions.
> 12 The sixth poured out his bowl on the great river Euphrates, and its water was dried up to prepare the way for the kings from the east.

The plagues demonstrated that Satan cannot withstand the power of God's judgment. Each of the plagues give us insight into Satan's domain that we can apply today. His kingdom is disgusting and God will clean up the mess.

The first plague was upon those who had the mark of the Beast and those who had worshiped his statue. They got big ugly sores. The False Prophet coerced almost everyone to go along, so they could stay in business.[54] Most people probably thought that the mark of the Beast was a good thing; it helped business. But then almost everyone got the sores. In the sixth sign,[55] an angel proclaimed that eternal torment is the ultimate fate of those who worship the Beast, worship his image, and receive his mark. But believers will be steadfast in the faith and will persevere in obeying God.

In our study of chapter 13, we applied the mark of the Beast to the influence of materialism in society today. Advertising convinces people to buy, buy, buy! When the money runs out, people resort to credit cards. Pretty soon the debt load is overwhelming, destroying lives, like the painful sores of the first plague. A credit card is merely a symbol of the materialism behind it. Other kinds of consumer debt are just as dangerous, such as payday loans, auto loans, student

---

[54] 13:16–17.
[55] 14:9–12.

loans, home equity loans, and so on. In the end, Satan's prosperity leads to suffering.

The second plague caused all the sea to become coagulated blood. The sea was the source of the Beast, Satan's agent of power.[56]

In our study of chapter 13, we applied the picture of the Beast to the power of modern States, which easily oppress their people. The blood-filled sea reminds us that worldly governments cannot bring life to their people. No matter how idealistic the politicians may sound, the result is oppression. Satan's power is lifeless.

The third plague polluted all the drinking water. The rivers and springs flowed with blood. Drinking blood is pretty disgusting. An angel speaking for creation said that this plague was appropriate, because the world had murdered believers.

Clean drinking water is essential for good health. One can't survive without it. We can apply the symbol of drinking water to spiritual health. Jesus said that he is the source of good drinking water, meaning the Holy Spirit.[57] The Holy Spirit enables one to live in righteousness, peace, and joy.[58] Satan's life is polluted and disgusting, because of the blood of martyrs.

The fourth plague scorched mankind with intense sunlight. There was no cloud cover to escape the sun's heat. People got fiery sunburns.

This plague reminds us that God hates sin like the intense heat of the sun. He will not just forget about it. There is no shade from the heat of God's wrath.

In the introduction of the bowls of plagues, the saints in heaven asked the rhetorical question, "Who shall not fear thee, O Lord, and glorify thy name?"[59] They couldn't imagine that mankind would continue its rebellion, but even after four devastating plagues, mankind cursed the name of the Lord and would not repent.

The fifth plague brought darkness and pain to the capital of the Beast and all of his domain. It had seemed like such a glamorous place, and now they only cursed God. They still would not repent.

> For though they knew God, they did not glorify Him as God or show gratitude. Instead, their thinking became nonsense, and their senseless minds were darkened. Claiming to be wise, they became fools and exchanged the glory of the immortal God for images resembling mortal man, birds, four-footed animals, and reptiles.
> Romans 1:21–23 (HCSB)

Even though Western civilization has a Christian heritage, the intelligentsia of today have ignored God and made mortal man the center of all things. They talk about sophisticated philosophies, but seem to live by slogans on bumper stickers. As a result, pessimism, selfishness, and violence permeate modern society and popular culture. The world's way of thinking is darkness.

---

[56] 13:1.
[57] John 4:14 and John 7:37–39.
[58] Romans 14:17.
[59] 15:4 (KJV).

The sixth plague caused the Euphrates River to dry up. It was no longer a barrier to the kings of the East. The Euphrates River was the traditional eastern border of the land Israel.[60] Without such a barrier, Israel would be open to invasions from the east. A border can represent protection and security. A natural barrier inhibits enemies from invading. The drying up of the Euphrates is like losing one's sense of security. Borders are insecure.

Several of these plagues also have parallels with the plagues on Egypt in Exodus.

- The first plague corresponds to sores on the Egyptians.[61]
- The third plague corresponds to turning the Nile River into blood.[62]
- The fifth plague corresponds to darkness over Egypt.[63]

Egypt's gods, the Nile and the sun, could not deliver them from the Lord's plagues. Satan could not prevent a plague of sores on his followers nor a plague of darkness in his own capital. The purpose of the plagues on Egypt was to demonstrate God's power, and to show that he alone is God.[64] Similarly, the purpose of these plagues was to demonstrate that God is much more powerful than Satan and his forces.

Several of these plagues have parallels with corresponding trumpets in chapters 8 and 9.

- The second plague corresponds to the second trumpet when one third of the sea became blood.[65]
- The third plague corresponds to the third trumpet when one third of the rivers and springs were poisoned.[66]
- The sixth plague corresponds to the sixth trumpet when one third of mankind was killed by the four destructive angels associated with the Euphrates River.[67]

When the trumpets made a call to repentance, only portions of creation were destroyed. The call to repentance was a foretaste of what God's wrath would be like. Here, the wrath of God affected entire aspects of creation. This was not the first time that God's judgment affected creation. Noah's Flood affected all of the land. Only Noah and the others in the ark were preserved. Here, those who did not follow the Beast were preserved.

---

[60] Genesis 15:18 and Deuteronomy 11:24.
[61] Exodus 9:8–12.
[62] Exodus 7:17–25.
[63] Exodus 10:21–23.
[64] Exodus 9:14–16.
[65] 8:8–9.
[66] 8:10–11.
[67] 9:13–19.

The Wrath of God

FOR PERSONAL STUDY
Six Bowls (16:1–12)

1. What sin is associated with the first plague? How does the plague fit the sin?

2. What is the main idea of the comments in verses 5–7?

3. What sin is associated with the third plague? How does the plague fit the sin?

4. What was the overall impact of these plagues on human life?

5. What was the reaction of mankind to the plagues? What should have been their reaction?

6. What would have been your reaction?

Gathering for War

> Why do the nations rebel and the peoples plot in vain? The kings of the earth take their stand, and the rulers conspire together against the Lord and His Anointed One: "Let us tear off their chains and free ourselves from their restraints."
>
> Psalms 2:1–3 (HCSB)

I can imagine the scene when Jesus has returned in glory and is about to start his reign. The United Nations Security Council is in an emergency meeting. Frantic negotiations are going on behind closed doors. Someone says, "A unified stand is the only way to defeat this threat." "We can't allow this intruder to take over." "It is unanimous. Meet at the hill by the river."

Read this section's Scripture passage.

Revelation 16:13–16 (HCSB)

---

13 Then I saw three unclean spirits like frogs coming from the dragon's mouth, from the beast's mouth, and from the mouth of the false prophet. 14 For they are spirits of demons performing signs, who travel to the kings of the whole world to assemble them for the battle of the great day of God, the Almighty.

15 "Look, I am coming like a thief. The one who is alert and remains clothed so that he may not go around naked and people see his shame is blessed."

16 So they assembled them at the place called in Hebrew, Armagedon.

The scene changes with the phrase *And I saw* ... This passage is an interlude between the sixth and seventh plagues, like the interludes of the seven seals, the seven trumpets, and the seven signs.

The three main characters on Satan's side of the war have been the dragon, who is Satan himself, the Beast, who is his agent of power, and the False Prophet, who is his agent of deception. From each of these came a demon spirit. Their mission was to gather all the leaders of the world together to fight against the Lord. This coming battle is called *that great day of God, the Almighty* and the *battle of Armageddon*. The Great Day is when God will judge Satan and his demons.[68] Anyone who wants to be on Satan's side should show up at Armageddon to get in on the action.

John called the gathering place by a Hebrew name, *Armageddon*, which is translated *hill of Megiddo*.[69] In ancient times, Megiddo was a city in the plain of Esdraelon in northern Israel.[70] Its name is translated *place of troops*.[71] Joshua conquered the Canaanite king of Megiddo,[72] however the tribe of Manasseh did not take possession of the city from the Canaanites.[73] Deborah won a victory over the kings of Canaan there.[74] Many years later, Josiah, King of Judah, was killed there in a foolish battle.[75]

The name Armageddon emphasizes to us that Satan's forces will gather for battle at the "place of troops" and will be completely defeated, just as the Canaanites were defeated by Deborah. Satan's forces, gathering for battle, may seem invincible, but Jesus will come unexpectedly. We are to be ready and alert.

> Therefore be alert, since you don't know what day your Lord is coming. But know this: If the homeowner had known what time the thief was coming, he would have stayed alert and not let his house be broken into. This is why you also must be ready, because the Son of Man is coming at an hour you do not expect.
> Matthew 24:42–44 (HCSB)

FOR PERSONAL STUDY
Three Frogs   (16:13–16)

1. What kind of feeling does the picture of frogs add to the scene, rather than just saying "demons"?

---

[68] Jude 1:6.
[69] Lockyer, ed., s.v. *Armageddon*.
[70] Also known as the Jezreel Valley.
[71] Benjamin Davidson, *The Analytical Hebrew and Chaldee Lexicon* (Grand Rapids, Michigan: Zondervan, 1970), s.v. *Megiddo*. Originally published by Samuel Bagster, second edition, 1850.
[72] Joshua 12:21.
[73] Joshua 17:11–12 and Judges 1:27.
[74] Judges 5:19.
[75] 2 Chronicles 35:20–24, 2 Kings 23:29–30, and Zechariah 12:10–11.

The Hail Storm

Read Exodus 9:13–35.

And there fell upon men a great hail out of heaven, every stone about the weight of a talent: and men blasphemed God because of the plague of the hail; for the plague thereof was exceeding great.

Revelation 16:21 (KJV)

"That was sure some hail storm last night. It was so heavy that the neighbor's cattle were all killed, and the field hand died, too," an Egyptian farmer might have said.

"I'm sure glad I paid attention, when that Moses fellow said we'd better bring the livestock inside. He was telling the Pharaoh just yesterday to let those Hebrews leave the country, or else we'd have the biggest hail ever. I brought the cattle in, just in case, and we did have the biggest hail ever.

"That fellow Moses must have a pretty big God. I heard that the Pharaoh was almost convinced, too, but dug in his heels at the last minute. He just won't give in.

"As for me, I think I'll do whatever Moses' God says. There's no sense in getting in trouble when you don't have to. That was sure some hail storm last night."

PRAYER: Dear God, I'm sorry I'm so stubborn. Please help me to be tender-hearted toward you. Amen.

2. Why do you suppose Satan wants to gather the kings of the earth together?

3. Review Judges 4:1–5:31. Note the reference to Meggido in Judges 5:19. What do you expect to happen to the kings Satan gathered?

Finished

> When Jesus had received the sour wine, He said, "It is finished!" Then bowing His head, He gave up His spirit.
> John 19:30 (HCSB)

When Jesus died on the cross, God's plan for saving mankind was completed. The penalty for sin had been paid. Justice had been served. Mercy was available to all.

Read the remainder of chapter 16 of Revelation.

Revelation 16:17–21 (HCSB)

> 17 Then the seventh poured out his bowl into the air, and a loud voice came out of the sanctuary from the throne, saying, "It is done!" 18 There were flashes of lightning and rumblings of thunder. And a severe earthquake occurred like no other since man has been on the earth—so great was the quake. 19 The great city split into three parts, and the cities of the nations fell. Babylon the Great was remembered in God's presence; He gave her the cup filled with the wine of His fierce anger. 20 Every island fled, and the mountains disappeared. 21 Enormous hailstones, each weighing about 100 pounds, fell from the sky on people, and they blasphemed God for the plague of hail because that plague was extremely severe.

When the seventh plague was poured out, God's anger against mankind's sin was completed. God proclaimed, "It is done," and made his point with displays of his power: lightning, thunder, an earthquake, and a hailstorm.

When the seventh trumpet sounded, there was praise in heaven, because the Lord has begun to reign. This was followed by the Holy of Holies opening up accompanied by these same displays of power: lightning, thunder, earthquake, and hail.[76]

The fifth sign was an angel proclaiming, "Babylon is fallen."[77] This is fulfilled here, and is explained further in chapter 17. God remembered to give Babylon the cup of his wrath.

Just as Pharaoh would not repent,[78] mankind continued to curse God, rather than repent. Before God brought the plague of lightning, thunder, and hail

---
[76] 11:19.
[77] 14:8 (KJV).
[78] Exodus 9:27–35.

on Egypt, Moses warned the Egyptians to protect their livestock.[79] Throughout the centuries, God has been warning mankind to repent from sin, and to escape the plagues of his wrath. God has judged sin.

FOR PERSONAL STUDY
The Seventh Bowl   (16:17–21)

1. Summarize this plague in a single phrase. What do the disasters have in common?

2. How do the plagues emphasize the finality of the proclamation "It is done"?

3. How did the men on earth feel about it?

4. How will you feel when Jesus has finished his judgment?

Review

We are in a war. Satan is trying to destroy God's people, but God is sovereign. He will preserve his own and will judge sin.

In chapters 12 through 16 of Revelation, John saw visions which we can divide into seven signs. To apply these signs to our lives, let us look for parallels between the spiritual battles we face and those described in the signs.

The seventh sign was special. Seven angels in heaven were each given a bowl. As the angels poured out the wrath of God onto the Earth, John saw visions of plagues on the Earth. Let us first review the seven plagues to see the seventh sign as a whole. These are the applications which we have drawn from the seven plagues.

1. Satan's prosperity leads to suffering.

2. Satan's power is lifeless.

3. Satan's life is polluted and disgusting, because of the blood of martyrs.

4. There is no shade from the heat of God's wrath.

5. The world's way of thinking is darkness.

6. Borders are insecure.

7. God has judged sin.

---
[79] Exodus 9:18–26.

The plagues demonstrated what Satan is really offering mankind—only suffering. There is no escaping the just anger of the Lord God against the world's way of sin.

Even though it was obvious who is going to win this war, mankind did not repent. They cursed God over and over. We have seven good reasons not to join Satan's side of the battle. When Satan would tempt us to turn away from Jesus with the attractions of fame, fortune, intellect, and power, these plagues remind us of what Satan really is offering. Pain will increase instead of riches. Lifeless chaos will reign instead of power. Murder will spread instead of life. Wrath will erupt instead of peace. Confusion will blanket instead of clear thinking. Invaders will attack instead of security. Final judgment is guaranteed instead of immortality. Who would want Satan's kind of life? I'd rather follow Jesus.

> The one who believes in the Son has eternal life, but the one who refuses to believe in the Son will not see life; instead, the wrath of God remains on him.
>
> John 3:36 (HCSB)

The Father wants everyone to believe in his Son. The person who rejects him is asking for trouble. Being good most of the time doesn't compensate for ignoring God's Son. The lifestyle of a person who rejects Jesus degenerates, and becomes characterized by sexual immorality, impure thoughts and actions, and greed. These are the kinds of things that God gets angry about. God hates sin.[80] Sin is pretty common these days. Is anybody worried? Is anybody expecting God to get mad? Paul made it clear that no one has an excuse, irrespective of whether one has thought about God today. The fact God hates sin is obvious.[81] However, Jesus died on the cross for us. The fact God loves sinners is obvious, too.

Like the first sign, the seventh was a sign in heaven. The spiritual battle is ultimately won from God's vantage point. The ultimate weapon of spiritual warfare is God's wrath against sin.

Now let us consider the other signs. What is the overall message of the seven signs? The key to interpreting the seven signs is to see the spiritual battle and the forces on each side.

1. Satan, the dragon, hates God's people.

2. The agents of Satan, the Beast and the False Prophet, are making war against God's people.

3. Unrestrained worship is a spiritual weapon.

4. Preaching the gospel is a spiritual weapon.

5. Proclaiming "Babylon is fallen" is a spiritual weapon.

---

[80]Ephesians 5:5–6.
[81]Romans 1:18–20.

6. Steadfastness against the ways of the world is a spiritual weapon.

7. God's wrath against sin is the ultimate spiritual weapon.

On one side of the battle line are Satan, the Beast, and the False Prophet. Worldly power and religion are his agents. Their spiritual weapons are hatred, coercion, and deception.

On the other side are God the Father, Jesus, and his servants here on earth who have the Holy Spirit inside. Our weapons are worship, preaching the gospel, recognizing that society is fallen, refusing to be identified with the world, and the assurance that God will judge sin.

All of us are engaged in spiritual warfare whether we acknowledge it or not. The Holy Spirit within marks each of us as a target for Satan's forces. Our weapons of spiritual warfare enable us to live victoriously from day to day, even though the devil is angry.

FOR PERSONAL STUDY
Review—Seven Signs   (12:1–16:21)

1. Review the literal picture of each plague. (16:1–12,17–21)

2. What is the main idea of the seven bowls? (15:1–16:21)

3. How does the introduction (15:1–8) contribute to the main idea of the seven bowls?

4. How does the interlude (16:13–16) contribute to the main idea of the seven bowls?

5. Review the main idea of each of the first six signs (12:1–14:20).

6. What do the seven signs tell us about Satan's plans? What is he trying to do?

7. What do the seven signs tell us about God's plans? Which aspects are emphasized here?

8. What is the reaction of the world's people to God's plans?

9. What can you do to prepare for Satan's attacks?

The Real Superhero

> And behold, I am coming quickly. Blessed is he who heeds the words of the prophecy of this book.[a]
>
> Revelation 22:7 (NASB)

One afternoon, Grandma began to tell two boys about Jesus coming again.

They had seen spaceships, transporter beams, galactic battles, and superheros on Saturday morning TV. Such adventures are pretty exciting when you are ten years old. Of course, they knew it is all make-believe on Saturday morning TV.

As she told the story, their eyes got big. This was better than TV. Jesus will come in the clouds. The dead will rise. Believers will go up. Satan is the great galactic foe. Jesus is the true superhero.

Jesus might come any moment. There was no time to lose. They wanted to be on the winning side. There was no hesitation when she asked, "Do you want to ask him into your life?" Both said, "Yes," and began a lifelong adventure with Jesus.

> PRAYER: Jesus, thank you for coming into my life. Life with you is certainly exciting. Amen.

---

[a] Sixth beatitude of Revelation.

5

Victory

> His glory is great through Your victory; You confer majesty and splendor on him. You give him blessings forever; You cheer him with joy in Your presence. For the king relies on the Lord; through the faithful love of the Most High he is not shaken.
>
> Psalms 21:5–7 (HCSB)

In this psalm, David thanked God for victory over his enemies. However, the references to eternal things indicate that this psalm is also applicable to the Messiah's victory over his enemies. We can identify with the feelings of this psalm as we consider Jesus' victory.

This chapter focuses on the Lord's victory over Satan's forces. This is not just of academic interest, because we can begin living in the Lord's victory even before it is completed at the end of the age.

As shown in the following outline, chapter 17 through the first part of chapter 22 describes the victory that God has planned for us. We have outlined seven victories, that is, seven aspects of victory. Even though the visions are not explicitly numbered, as the seven seals were, in each case, John saw something new in a new setting. These chapters give us a complete picture of the Lord's victory.

IV. Seven-Fold Victory

1. The Fall of Babylon	17:1–19:10
2. Beasts Defeated	19:11–21
3. The Dragon Bound	20:1–10
4. Judgment	20:11–15
5. A New Heaven and New Earth	21:1–8
6. The New Jerusalem	21:9–27
7. The River of Life	22:1–5

Illustration 5.1: Babylon (17:1–19:21)

The Fall of Civilization

On the night of August 24, AD 410, Alaric, King of the Visigoths, led one hundred thousand Goths through the Salarian gate and sacked the city of Rome.[1] Rome had ruled the world for centuries, and seemed to be the foundation of civilization. Saint Jerome wrote to a friend, "What is safe if Rome perishes?" Even though the Western empire continued for a while, many thought the end of the world was imminent.[2]

The prostitute. Over three hundred years before, John saw a vision of the destruction of Babylon, representing the Rome of his day. Read chapter 17 of Revelation.

Revelation 17:1–18 (HCSB)

1 Then one of the seven angels who had the seven bowls came and spoke with me: "Come, I will show you the judgment of the notorious prostitute who sits on many waters. 2 The kings of the earth committed sexual immorality with her, and those who live on the earth became drunk on the wine of her sexual immorality." 3 So he carried me away in the Spirit to a desert. I saw a woman sitting on a scarlet beast that was covered with blasphemous names and had seven heads and 10 horns. 4 The woman was dressed in purple and scarlet, adorned with gold, precious stones, and pearls. She had a gold cup in her hand filled with everything vile and with the impurities of her prostitution. 5 On her forehead a cryptic name was written:

BABYLON THE GREAT
THE MOTHER OF PROSTITUTES
AND OF THE VILE THINGS OF THE EARTH.

6 Then I saw that the woman was drunk on the blood of the saints and on the blood of the witnesses to Jesus. When I saw her, I was greatly astonished.

7 Then the angel said to me, "Why are you astonished? I will tell you the secret meaning of the woman and of the beast, with the seven heads and the 10 horns, that carries her. 8 The beast that you saw was, and is not, and is about to come up from the abyss and go to destruction. Those who live on the earth whose names have not been written in the book of life from the foundation of the world will be astonished when they see the beast that was, and is not, and will be present again.

---

[1] Otto Friedrich, *The End of the World* (New York: Coward, McCann and Geoghegan, 1982), p. 57.
[2] Friedrich, p. 27.

9 "Here is the mind with wisdom: The seven heads are seven mountains on which the woman is seated. 10 They are also seven kings: Five have fallen, one is, the other has not yet come, and when he comes, he must remain for a little while. 11 The beast that was and is not, is himself an eighth king, yet he belongs to the seven and is going to destruction. 12 The 10 horns you saw are 10 kings who have not yet received a kingdom, but they will receive authority as kings with the beast for one hour. 13 These have one purpose, and they give their power and authority to the beast. 14 These will make war against the Lamb, but the Lamb will conquer them because He is Lord of lords and King of kings. Those with Him are called, chosen, and faithful."

15 He also said to me, "The waters you saw, where the prostitute was seated, are peoples, multitudes, nations, and languages. 16 The 10 horns you saw, and the beast, will hate the prostitute. They will make her desolate and naked, devour her flesh, and burn her up with fire. 17 For God has put it into their hearts to carry out His plan by having one purpose and to give their kingdom to the beast until God's words are accomplished. 18 And the woman you saw is the great city that has an empire over the kings of the earth."

Chapter 17 through the first part of chapter 19 describes the victory over Babylon. Having seen the seven signs, including the wrath of God completely poured out on sin, John was probably wondering what it all meant. In the next vision, one of the angels who had poured out a bowl showed John more details about the fall of Babylon and the cup of God's wrath given to Babylon.[3]

After seeing a prostitute riding on a beast, John was puzzled, just like the rest of us. Much of Revelation is hard to understand upon first reading. The figurative language is difficult. The symbols are unfamiliar. The scenes are hard to visualize. However, in this case, the angel promised John an explanation. God's ways are the same regarding the entire book. He wants us to understand it and apply it to our lives, and he will give us the information necessary to do the job. The passage itself gives us the primary interpretation. A cross reference to another scripture may emphasize a point, but the basics are right here.

Who was the great prostitute?

The answer is "the great city that has an empire over the kings of the earth."[4] In John's time, the greatest city in the world was obviously Rome. Her name was also written on her forehead: Babylon. This name is a symbol also, telling us that the character of this great city is like that of ancient Babylon.

We can apply this picture of Babylon to Western Civilization today, which has its roots in the Roman culture of John's time. Western Civilization has become the dominant civilization of Earth. It is characterized by idolatry of

---

[3] 14:8 and 16:19.
[4] 17:18 (HCSB).

wealth and material prosperity. Even those countries which do not have a Western heritage are envious of the material prosperity of Western Civilization, and try to imitate it. Some have adopted Western materialism very quickly.

Who was the Beast?

The answer is the beast from the sea, described in chapter 13. In both visions, John saw a beast with seven heads and ten horns, with blasphemous names.[5] This passage describes the Beast in detail.[6]

What were the seven heads of the Beast?

The answer is seven hills,[7] and also seven kings, plus an eighth king. In John's day, as today, Rome was famous for its seven hills. The kings remind us that Rome was the seat of government for the world at that time.

What were the ten horns of the Beast?

The answer is ten other kings. Evidently, the Beast does not represent a single historical person. Rather, he was a composite of spiritual forces, which acted through various kings.

As in chapter 13, we can apply the picture of the Beast to the power of the State. Throughout history, government has been a major instrument of power against the gospel.

Why did God judge the prostitute?

The answer is she was drunk with the blood of martyrs for Jesus.[8] Jeremiah prophesied against ancient Babylon in chapters 50 and 51, when it was the dominant world power.[9]

> Babylon must fall because of the slain of Israel, even as the slain of all the earth fell because of Babylon.
>
> Jeremiah 51:49 (HCSB)

God judged the ancient city, Babylon, because it had abused God's people, Israel. God judged the prostitute, Babylon, because she abused God's people, martyrs for Jesus. God will avenge the deaths of his people.[10] The prostitute had a gold cup, beautiful on the outside, but filthy on the inside. This picture of the "wine of the wrath of her fornication" clearly illustrates her actual character.[11]

Like the prostitute, Babylon, Western Civilization today has a cup full of materialism and sexual immorality. The media fawns over the rich and famous. Business is always in the news. One would think sex or economics explains everything. The outside of the cup may glitter and seem glamorous, but from God's point of view, the inside is filthy with idolatry and selfishness. Even though God's judgment of Western Civilization has not yet fallen, we can apply the passage as a warning to our times.

---

[5] 13:1.
[6] 17:8–12.
[7] 17:9 (NIV).
[8] 17:6, 18:20, and 19:2.
[9] A detailed study of Jeremiah 50–51 is outside the scope of this book.
[10] Deuteronomy 32:43.
[11] 14:8 (KJV) and 18:3.

Fallen. The alarm sounded. Everyone in the office stopped and looked at each other. Was this a drill or a real fire? No one dared ignore the sound. When we finally got to the bottom of the stairs, the fire trucks were out front and the firemen were on their way up. The fire alarm may have been inconvenient, but we were all glad to be safe outside.

God's alarm sounded. Read chapter 18 of Revelation.

Revelation 18:1–24 (HCSB)

> 1 After this I saw another angel with great authority coming down from heaven, and the earth was illuminated by his splendor. 2 He cried in a mighty voice:
>
>> It has fallen,
>> Babylon the Great has fallen!
>> She has become a dwelling for demons,
>> a haunt for every unclean spirit,
>> a haunt for every unclean bird,
>> and a haunt for every unclean and despicable beast.
>> 3 For all the nations have drunk
>> the wine of her sexual immorality,
>> which brings wrath.
>> The kings of the earth
>> have committed sexual immorality with her,
>> and the merchants of the earth
>> have grown wealthy from her excessive luxury.
>
> 4 Then I heard another voice from heaven:
>
>> Come out of her, My people,
>> so that you will not share in her sins
>> or receive any of her plagues.
>> 5 For her sins are piled up to heaven,
>> and God has remembered her crimes.
>> 6 Pay her back the way she also paid,
>> and double it according to her works.
>> In the cup in which she mixed,
>> mix a double portion for her.
>> 7 As much as she glorified herself and lived luxuriously,
>> give her that much torment and grief,
>> for she says in her heart,
>> "I sit as a queen;
>> I am not a widow,
>> and I will never see grief."
>> 8 For this reason her plagues will come in one day—
>> death and grief and famine.
>> She will be burned up with fire,
>> because the Lord God who judges her is mighty.

9 The kings of the earth who have committed sexual immorality and lived luxuriously with her will weep and mourn over her when they see the smoke of her burning. 10 They will stand far off in fear of her torment, saying:

> Woe, woe, the great city,
> Babylon, the mighty city!
> For in a single hour
> your judgment has come.

11 The merchants of the earth will also weep and mourn over her, because no one buys their merchandise any longer— 12 merchandise of gold, silver, precious stones, and pearls; fine fabrics of linen, purple, silk, and scarlet; all kinds of fragrant wood products; objects of ivory; objects of expensive wood, brass, iron, and marble; 13 cinnamon, spice, incense, myrrh, and frankincense; wine, olive oil, fine wheat flour, and grain; cattle and sheep; horses and carriages; and slaves and human lives.

> 14 The fruit you craved has left you.
> All your splendid and glamorous things are gone;
> they will never find them again.

15 The merchants of these things, who became rich from her, will stand far off in fear of her torment, weeping and mourning, 16 saying:

> Woe, woe, the great city,
> dressed in fine linen, purple, and scarlet,
> adorned with gold, precious stones, and pearls,
> 17 for in a single hour
> such fabulous wealth was destroyed!

And every shipmaster, seafarer, the sailors, and all who do business by sea, stood far off 18 as they watched the smoke from her burning and kept crying out: "Who is like the great city?" 19 They threw dust on their heads and kept crying out, weeping, and mourning:

> Woe, woe, the great city,
> where all those who have ships on the sea
> became rich from her wealth,
> for in a single hour she was destroyed.
> 20 Rejoice over her, heaven,
> and you saints, apostles, and prophets,
> because God has executed your judgment on her!

21 Then a mighty angel picked up a stone like a large millstone and threw it into the sea, saying:

> In this way, Babylon the great city
> will be thrown down violently

> and never be found again.
> 22 The sound of harpists, musicians,
> flutists, and trumpeters
> will never be heard in you again;
> no craftsman of any trade
> will ever be found in you again;
> the sound of a mill
> will never be heard in you again;
> 23 the light of a lamp
> will never shine in you again;
> and the voice of a groom and bride
> will never be heard in you again.
> All this will happen
> because your merchants
> were the nobility of the earth,
> because all the nations were deceived
> by your sorcery,
> 24 and the blood of prophets and saints,
> and of all those slaughtered on earth,
> was found in you.

God called to his people to leave the great city, the prostitute Babylon, so that they would not be affected by God's judgment against her. Jeremiah made a similar call to Israel when he prophesied against ancient Babylon.

> Come out from among her, My people! Save your lives, each of you, from the Lord's burning anger.
>
> Jeremiah 51:45 (HCSB)

We can apply this command to our lives by boycotting the ungodly lifestyle that is so common today.

> But know this: Difficult times will come in the last days. For people will be lovers of self, lovers of money, boastful, proud, blasphemers, disobedient to parents, ungrateful, unholy, unloving, irreconcilable, slanderers, without self-control, brutal, without love for what is good, traitors, reckless, conceited, lovers of pleasure rather than lovers of God, holding to the form of godliness but denying its power. Avoid these people!
>
> 2 Timothy 3:1–5 (HCSB)

This principle is relevant in small things as well as the big obvious things. For example, we get a lot of mail at our house. Most of it is advertising for things we would never use from stores that charge too much. The advertising appeals to pride, greed, and self indulgence. The underlying message is "You should buy this item to be a happy person." Of course, that is a lie. We avoid being tricked into such attitudes by throwing it away without even looking at it. If we maintain a godly lifestyle, then we will not be affected by God's judgment against the world's sin.

Paul made it clear that we should not try to segregate ourselves from society at large. It is impractical to avoid all the immoral, greedy, dishonest, idolatrous people in this world. Rather, we should not fellowship with the world as though they are believers.[12] We should love and relate to them as Jesus did.

God wants us to understand the symbols in Revelation, and so he explains the primary interpretation right here in the passage. Let's look at some more details about Babylon.

Who were the prostitute's partners?

The answer is "the kings of the earth."[13] The passage says that Babylon "committed adultery with the kings of the earth." Not only were the leaders involved, but merchants grew rich from her extravagance, and people in general were intoxicated with her immorality.

What were the "many waters" where the prostitute sat?

The answer is "peoples, multitudes, nations and languages."[14] Rome ruled over the civilized world, including many nationalities, ethnic groups, and language groups.

Adultery is often used in scripture to portray idolatry. The world should have been worshiping God, but instead people were worshiping all that Babylon represented: pride, materialism, desecration of sexuality, blasphemy, and murder of believers.

The politicians, businessmen, and traders mourned the fall of Babylon, but believers, apostles and prophets who were persecuted by her rejoiced. The politicians mourned because they aspired to the greatness that Babylon represented. All of the sudden, that greatness was destroyed. The businessmen and traders mourned because she supported their materialism and greed. This indicates the type of idolatry that Babylon spread around the world. The people of the world were intoxicated by the escapades in Babylon, like readers of a scintillating tabloid.

The destruction of Babylon was complete. It became so desolate that there was no music, no workshops, no industry, no lights, and no weddings. Jeremiah mentions these same things to describe Israel after their defeat.[15]

Hallelujah. On game day, the cheers from the grandstands were so loud you couldn't think. The stadium was packed to capacity. We all wanted to beat the rival school across town. The enthusiasm was thick in the air. This was not an accident. The day before the big game there had been a rally. Everyone at school had been there. The cheers grew louder and louder, so the grandstands would be ready on game day.

---

[12] 1 Corinthians 5:9–11 and 2 Corinthians 6:14–7:1.
[13] 17:2 and 18:3.
[14] 17:15 (HCSB).
[15] Jeremiah 25:10. This list is a formula which emphasizes the utter desolation.

A Wedding Invitation

Read Luke 14:16–24.

Blessed are those who are invited to the marriage supper of the Lamb.[a]

Revelation 19:9 (NASB)

The silver trimmed invitation had come a thousand miles. "We joyfully request your presence to witness before God and man . . . ," signed "Nancy and Bob." What a thrill it was to get that wedding invitation.

Jesus told a parable about a man who gave a big reception. Many people received special invitations, but each had an excuse. "I've just made a big business deal." "I have to work late tonight." "I'm on my honeymoon." They were just too busy.

So, he invited the poor, the handicapped, the homeless, and the transient to enjoy his banquet. He wanted everyone to come to the reception, but these were the ones who accepted the invitation. The hall was filled with celebrating guests who didn't even expect an invitation.

Jesus has extended his personal invitation to us. His wedding reception is more important than work, play, or family. Each of us has an invitation, even if we didn't expect one. It is an invitation to receive him into our lives.

> PRAYER: Lord, thank you for your invitation. Thank you for forgiving me, and for coming into my life. I'm looking forward to your wedding reception. Amen.

---

[a] Fourth beatitude of Revelation.

The Fall of Civilization

Heaven has grandstands, too. Read the first ten verses of chapter 19.

Revelation 19:1–10 (HCSB)

---

1 After this I heard something like the loud voice of a vast multitude in heaven, saying:

> Hallelujah!
> Salvation, glory, and power belong to our God,
> 2 because His judgments are true and righteous,
> because He has judged the notorious prostitute
> who corrupted the earth with her sexual immorality;
> and He has avenged the blood of His slaves
> that was on her hands.

3 A second time they said:

> Hallelujah!
> Her smoke ascends forever and ever!

4 Then the 24 elders and the four living creatures fell down and worshiped God, who is seated on the throne, saying:

> Amen! Hallelujah!

5 A voice came from the throne, saying:

> Praise our God,
> all His slaves, who fear Him,
> both small and great!

6 Then I heard something like the voice of a vast multitude, like the sound of cascading waters, and like the rumbling of loud thunder, saying:

> Hallelujah, because our Lord God, the Almighty,
> has begun to reign!
> 7 Let us be glad, rejoice, and give Him glory,
> because the marriage of the Lamb has come,
> and His wife has prepared herself.
> 8 She was given fine linen to wear, bright and pure.

For the fine linen represents the righteous acts of the saints.

9 Then he said to me, "Write: Those invited to the marriage feast of the Lamb are fortunate!" He also said to me, "These words of God are true." 10 Then I fell at his feet to worship him, but he said to me, "Don't do that! I am a fellow slave with you and your brothers who have the testimony about Jesus. Worship God, because the testimony about Jesus is the spirit of prophecy."

After the destruction of Babylon, the heavenly grandstands erupted with cheers. John heard praise from the multitude in heaven, and from the elders and creatures around the throne of God.[16]

We don't have to wait until we get to the heavenly grandstands to join the cheering. Every time evil is defeated and good prevails, we have reason to praise the Lord. Our praises today are like a pregame rally, preparing for that day in the grandstands around the throne.

After rejoicing over the fall of Babylon, a voice from God's throne called on everyone to praise God. First, the Lord God Almighty reigns, and second, the Lamb is getting married, and the bride is ready.

We already know from chapter 5 that the Lamb is interpreted as Jesus. Who is the bride of the Lamb?

> Husbands, love your wives, just as Christ loved the church and gave Himself for her to make her holy, cleansing her with the washing of water by the word. He did this to present the church to Himself in splendor, without spot or wrinkle or anything like that, but holy and blameless... This mystery is profound, but I am talking about Christ and the church.
>
> Ephesians 5:25–32 (HCSB)

Christ and the church have a relationship just like a bride and groom. Believers, taken as a group are like a bride and Jesus is like the groom. This passage in Revelation tells us that the wedding is scheduled.

Each husband and wife have a special opportunity to demonstrate what knowing Jesus is like. The relationship of my wife and I should follow the example of Christ in his relationship to us, the church. My love for her should be self-sacrificing for her benefit, doing all I can to encourage godly character in her. For example, we read a meditation and pray together at the breakfast table. As her husband, it is my responsibility to remember to do this regularly, because it helps her day get started right. (It helps my day, too.)

The bride had a beautiful white linen wedding dress. The wedding dress is interpreted for us. "The fine linen is the righteousness of saints."[17]

Righteousness is defined as the concrete expression of righteousness, for example a judicial sentence, or a righteous act.[18] *Young's Concordance* prefers the translation *judicial sentence*.[19] Because of the cross, the judicial sentence against us is "righteous" instead of "condemned." Righteousness is based on the grace of God through faith alone.[20] The *Holman Christian Standard Bible* and the *New American Standard Bible* both prefer the translation *righteous acts*.[21] Good works

---

[16] 7:9, 4:4, and 4:6.

[17] 19:8 (KJV).

[18] The Greek word translated *righteousness* is *dikaiomata*. Vine, s.v. righteousness.

[19] Robert Young, *Young's Analytical Concordance to the Bible*, revised by William B. Stevenson and David Wimbish (Nashville: Thomas Nelson, 1980) s.v. righteousness. This reference book includes brief definitions of Hebrew and Greek words, in addition to concordance references. It is an alternative to *Strong's* as a concordance.

[20] Romans 4:1–5 and Romans 3:22–24.

[21] 19:8 (HCSB).

are the practical result that righteousness has on our lives. That is the way God planned it.[22] The *Amplified Bible* includes both senses of the word.

> The righteousness—the upright, just and godly living [deeds, conduct] and right standing with God—of the saints.
> Revelation 19:8 (AB)

The white linen wedding dress of the bride reminds us of what Jesus did for us on the cross, and that our lives should put His righteousness into action.

Someone told John to write down a beatitude: "Blessed are they which are called unto the marriage supper of the Lamb."[23] John was so awe-struck that he fell down to worship the speaker. He was promptly corrected. The messenger was just another believer who was passing along what God has said.

When Jesus returns and his victory is complete, we can expect Western Civilization, with all its idolatry of material things to be completely destroyed, and for the righteousness of the church to shine instead.

The first victory is over the world system.

FOR PERSONAL STUDY
The Fall of Babylon (17:1–19:10)

1. List the characteristics of Babylon as if she were a person.

2. What aspects of your description are applicable to a city? ...to ancient Rome? ...to a modern city?

3. What sins of Babylon are emphasized in 18:1–7?

4. Are these sins common in your home town? ...in the nearest big city?

5. How are the pronouncements in 18:8 and 18:20–24 related to Babylon's sins?

6. Why are the kings, merchants, and traders mourning for Babylon? (18:9–19)

7. Why do God's people rejoice? (18:20)

8. How would you feel if the same thing happened to your home town?

9. What does 17:7–18 say about these symbols:
    - Scarlet beast?
    - Seven heads?
    - Ten horns?
    - Waters?

---
[22] James 2:17–18 and Ephesians 2:8–10.
[23] 19:9 (KJV).

- The woman?

10. What will God use to destroy Babylon?

11. List the characteristics of the Bride as a person?

12. How is the Bride different from Babylon?

13. Picture the scene in 19:1–10. Picture yourself in the middle of the crowd. Listen to a recording of "The Hallelujah Chorus" from Handel's *Messiah*, if possible, and meditate on its words (19:6 and 11:15).

The Defeat of Oppression

I was at the movie theater watching a Western. The good guys, the ones with white hats, were fighting the bad guys, the ones with black hats. The good guys were surrounded, and the situation looked bleak. Then suddenly, the cavalry appeared from over the hill, routed the enemy, and rescued all those with white hats.

Jesus has his cavalry, too. Read the remainder of chapter 19 of Revelation.

Revelation 19:11–21 (HCSB)

> 11 Then I saw heaven opened, and there was a white horse. Its rider is called Faithful and True, and He judges and makes war in righteousness. 12 His eyes were like a fiery flame, and many crowns were on His head. He had a name written that no one knows except Himself. 13 He wore a robe stained with blood, and His name is the Word of God. 14 The armies that were in heaven followed Him on white horses, wearing pure white linen. 15 A sharp sword came from His mouth, so that He might strike the nations with it. He will shepherd them with an iron scepter. He will also trample the winepress of the fierce anger of God, the Almighty. 16 And He has a name written on His robe and on His thigh:
>
>> KING OF KINGS
>> AND LORD OF LORDS.
>
> 17 Then I saw an angel standing on the sun, and he cried out in a loud voice, saying to all the birds flying high overhead, "Come, gather together for the great supper of God, 18 so that you may eat the flesh of kings, the flesh of commanders, the flesh of mighty men, the flesh of horses and of their riders, and the flesh of everyone, both free and slave, small and great."
>
> 19 Then I saw the beast, the kings of the earth, and their armies gathered together to wage war against the rider on the horse and against His army. 20 But the beast was taken prisoner, and along with him the false prophet, who had performed the signs in his

presence. He deceived those who accepted the mark of the beast and those who worshiped his image with these signs. Both of them were thrown alive into the lake of fire that burns with sulfur. 21 The rest were killed with the sword that came from the mouth of the rider on the horse, and all the birds were filled with their flesh.

Who is the rider of the white horse?

The answer is Jesus. The description brings together many symbols that have already appeared in Revelation, as well as some from other Scriptures. He was called the "faithful witness" in the vision which introduced the letters to the churches.[24] Throughout the gospels, Jesus claimed that his words were true. He said, "I am the way, the truth, and the life."[25] We can trust him to tell us the truth. Jesus had "eyes as a flame of fire" in the vision which introduced the letters to the churches.[26] The "robe dipped in blood" reminds us of his death on the cross. He is called "The Word" in the opening verses of the Gospel of John.[27] In verse 13 and in the Gospel of John, *Word* means the expression of thought.[28] The Son of God is the expression of the Father's thoughts. His thoughts about us are full of the love and compassion that Jesus showed during his time on earth.

The armies that followed Jesus might be believers, because they are dressed in white linen like the bride of Christ.[29]

The sword coming out of his mouth reminds us of the vision which introduced the letters to the churches.[30] "He will rule them with an iron scepter,"[31] is a quote of Psalms 2:9. In the first sign, it is prophesied that the child will rule the nations with a rod of iron.[32] Similarly, those who overcome will rule with Jesus with a rod of iron.[33] "The wine press of the wrath of God" was introduced in the interlude between the sixth and seventh signs.[34] Now we know it was Jesus treading that winepress. Earlier, the title "King of Kings and Lord of Lords" was given to the Lamb, Jesus.[35] The Son of God is the expression of the Father's thoughts. His thoughts about sin are true and just, strong and angry. He wields full authority over creation and mankind.

As the battle shaped up, an angel organized the cleanup crew. He called for birds to come eat the carnage of the battle. Jeremiah used a similar image to emphasize the complete slaughter and desolation of Judah.

---

[24] 1:5 and 3:14.
[25] John 14:6.
[26] 1:14 (KJV).
[27] John 1:1–3 and John 1:14–17.
[28] The Greek word for *Word* is *logos*. Vine, s.v. *Word*.
[29] 19:8.
[30] 1:16 and 2:12.
[31] 19:15 (NIV).
[32] 12:5.
[33] 2:27.
[34] 14:19–20.
[35] 17:14.

> The corpses of these people will become food for the birds of the sky and for the wild animals of the land, with no one to scare them away.
> Jeremiah 7:33 (HCSB)

The victims of this battle were all kinds of people, the same ones who had been deceived by the False Prophet. The small and great, rich and poor, free and slaves, all had received the mark of the Beast.[36] In the interlude between the sixth and seventh plagues, Satan's demons gathered the kings of the Earth together for battle.[37] Also, the ten horns of the Beast represented kings who will fight the Lamb.[38]

The culmination of this victory is the complete destruction of the Beast and the False Prophet.[39] They were thrown into the lake of fire.[40] The rest of their followers were judged by the word of God which came from Jesus' mouth.

> The one who rejects Me and doesn't accept My sayings has this as his judge: The word I have spoken will judge him on the last day.
> John 12:48 (HCSB)

Those who reject Jesus act as though he is lying. He does love each one and wants to save each one. However, those who reject his good news of love are, in effect, standing with the Beast and False Prophet, calling him a liar. They will one day find out that he did tell the truth.

The Beast had been the instrument of Satan's oppressive power. The False Prophet had been the instrument of Satan's deception of the whole world, convincing them to worship the Beast rather than the Lord. They were defeated forever.

Even though oppression still runs rampant today, we look forward with confidence to the defeat of Satan's forces. Even though propaganda is taken as gospel, we see the truth clearly. Confidence in the face of oppression and clarity in the face of deception show the world that the defeat of Satan's forces is inevitable.

The second victory is over worldly power.

FOR PERSONAL STUDY
Beasts Defeated   (19:11–21)

1. What roles of Jesus are emphasized by the symbols of verses 11–16?

2. Review 13:1–18. What did the Beast and False Prophet do to deserve their punishment?

---

[36] 13:16.
[37] 16:14,16.
[38] 17:13–14.
[39] 13:1,11 and 16:13.
[40] In Matthew 10:28 the lake of fire is called *Gehenna*, the Hebrew word denoting everlasting destruction, which is transliterated in the Greek New Testament (*Strong's* No. 1067).

3. How were the Beast and False Prophet defeated? How does their sin fit the way they were defeated?

4. Review forces in your life that are like the Beast and the False Prophet. Describe some incidents where they have been defeated.

5. What is a good strategy for dealing with forces like the Beast and False Prophet?

6. Who were enlisted in the army of the Beast and False Prophet? What happened to them?

FOR PERSONAL STUDY
Washing Feet (John 13:1–16)

Read John 13:1–16. The Bride of Christ, the Church, is described as "arrayed in fine linen ... the righteousness of the saints."[41] One example of this righteousness is when one Christian serves another in a humble way.

1. Describe what Jesus did in this passage. Why was this commonplace in their society at that time?

2. How did this show Jesus' love for His disciples?

3. Why was Peter surprised?

4. What is the main idea that Jesus was trying to teach the disciples?

5. What are some modern actions that are like washing feet in Jesus' time?

6. If we want to follow Jesus' example, what kind of relationships should we have with each other?

The End of Deception

The kids seemed spellbound as the magician did his act. "Wow! How did he do that?" The older kids knew his marvels were only illusions, but were just as mesmerized, trying to figure them out. As long as the trick was a secret, he had them, but he lost his power as soon as the trick was explained.

---

[41] 19:8 (KJV).

Illustration 5.2: Satan Bound (20:1–10)

The End of Deception

Satan bound. Read this section's passage about the Great Deceiver.

Revelation 20:1–10 (HCSB)

---

1 Then I saw an angel coming down from heaven with the key to the abyss and a great chain in his hand. 2 He seized the dragon, that ancient serpent who is the Devil and Satan, and bound him for 1,000 years. 3 He threw him into the abyss, closed it, and put a seal on it so that he would no longer deceive the nations until the 1,000 years were completed. After that, he must be released for a short time.

4 Then I saw thrones, and people seated on them who were given authority to judge. I also saw the people who had been beheaded because of their testimony about Jesus and because of God's word, who had not worshiped the beast or his image, and who had not accepted the mark on their foreheads or their hands. They came to life and reigned with the Messiah for 1,000 years. 5 The rest of the dead did not come to life until the 1,000 years were completed. This is the first resurrection. 6 Blessed and holy is the one who shares in the first resurrection! The second death has no power over them, but they will be priests of God and of the Messiah, and they will reign with Him for 1,000 years.

7 When the 1,000 years are completed, Satan will be released from his prison 8 and will go out to deceive the nations at the four corners of the earth, Gog and Magog, to gather them for battle. Their number is like the sand of the sea. 9 They came up over the surface of the earth and surrounded the encampment of the saints, the beloved city. Then fire came down from heaven and consumed them. 10 The Devil who deceived them was thrown into the lake of fire and sulfur where the beast and the false prophet are, and they will be tormented day and night forever and ever.

John saw an angel throw Satan into jail for one thousand years. This prevented him from deceiving anyone. Satan's name, *that ancient serpent*, reminds us of the Garden of Eden, where Satan, in the form of a snake, lied to the woman. He is a deceiver. He has been lying ever since.

With Satan out of the way, life on earth was much better. Jesus was in charge. We don't have to wait for Jesus to return to see Satan defeated. We just have to be wary of Satan's lies in everyday life. He loses his power as soon as his tricks are explained. If we live honestly with a biblically accurate view of the world, then life on earth will be much better. We don't have to wait for Jesus to return to know he is in charge. We can submit our lives to him from day to day.[42]

---

[42] Romans 12:1–2.

The millennium. Believers were resurrected and ruled with Jesus for a thousand years. Those seated on thrones remind us of the trials that believers have had. Some have been killed.[43] Some have refused to worship idols.[44] Some have refused to belong to the world system.[45] This resurrection was for overcomers.[46]

Theologians have argued for centuries over the detailed interpretation of the one thousand years mentioned in chapter 20, the "millennium." Is the passage literal or figurative? Will Jesus return before or after? Rather than get embroiled in a theological controversy, let us focus on a lesson for today.

The first death is when our physical bodies quit working. We are comforted, because the resurrection of Jesus is the guarantee that believers too will be resurrected to everlasting life.[47]

The final deception. A freshman in college encounters many new ideas. I was far from home, and far from the church I grew up in. I met many intelligent people who did not believe in Jesus like I did. We would talk late into the night about philosophy and life. It was quite a challenge, but I found that the principles in the Bible made much more sense than their convoluted arguments.

> Be careful that no one takes you captive through philosophy and empty deceit based on human tradition, based on the elemental forces of the world, and not based on Christ.
> Colossians 2:8 (HCSB)

When the thousand-year reign was over, there was still some unfinished business in God's plan. Satan had one last chance to deceive the nations and lead a rebellion. It's amazing that anyone would believe him after a thousand years of peace and prosperity.

He deceived nations from all over the Earth. Gog and Magog are mentioned specifically. Magog was a grandson of Noah who settled far from Palestine.[48] Ezekiel prophesied against Gog who was from the land of Magog.[49] He was a prince over some of Magog's brothers, and had other nations in his army.[50] This just further emphasizes that Satan deceived nations from all over the Earth, even remote places.

When Satan's soldiers besieged Jesus' capital, Jerusalem, they were confident that they would win. They lost. God's arsenal of fire from heaven destroyed them. Satan's last stand had failed miserably. Satan, the deceiver, was thrown into the lake of fire to be tormented forever.

---

[43] 2:10,13.
[44] 13:15.
[45] 13:16–17.
[46] 2:11.
[47] 1 Corinthians 15:51–57.
[48] Genesis 10:2.
[49] A detailed study of Ezekiel 38:1–39:29 is beyond the scope of this book.
[50] Ezekiel 38:1–5.

Many people today are tricked by Satan into joining his rebellion against God. Some say God does not exist. Others think God is dead, or perhaps just far away. Some say, "I don't know," but act the same as the atheist. Some don't care about philosophy, and just mind their own business. Without knowing it, they too have joined his rebellion.

With the Deceiver in jail, Jesus will demonstrate what the Earth can be like under righteous reign. He will demonstrate what God intended when he made heaven and Earth. Finally, Jesus will complete God's plan for the Earth by finally destroying Satan and his forces.

The third victory is over Satan.

> For as in Adam all die, so also in Christ all will be made alive. But each in his own order: Christ, the firstfruits; afterward, at His coming, those who belong to Christ. Then comes the end, when He hands over the kingdom to God the Father, when He abolishes all rule and all authority and power. For He must reign until He puts all His enemies under His feet.
>
> 1 Corinthians 15:22–25 (HCSB)

FOR PERSONAL STUDY
The Dragon Bound   (20:1–10)

1. Review Satan's activities in chapters 12 and 13. Why is Satan bound?

2. List the characteristics of those who share the one thousand years with Jesus?

3. What was Satan hoping to accomplish after he was released? Describe what happened in your own words.

4. What are some of the ways Satan has tricked you?

5. What helps you to keep alert and to see through Satan's tricks?

The Last Enemy

> After the Sabbath, as the first day of the week was dawning, Mary Magdalene and the other Mary went to view the tomb. Suddenly there was a violent earthquake, because an angel of the Lord descended from heaven and approached the tomb. He rolled back the stone and was sitting on it. His appearance was like lightning, and his robe was as white as snow. The guards were so shaken from fear of him that they became like dead men. But the angel told the women, "Don't be afraid, because I know you are looking for Jesus who was crucified. He is not here! For He has been resurrected, just as He said. Come and see the place where He lay."
>
> Matthew 28:1–6 (HCSB)

A New Housecoat

> Blessed and holy is the one who has a part in the first resurrection; over these the second death has no power.[a]
> Revelation 20:6 (NASB)

Faye was forty-eight years old when she learned that she had cancer and it had spread into the lymph system.

Late one night, alone in her hospital room, tears streamed down her face. Even though she felt the Lord close by, she still didn't like the prospect of dying. She was planning on that mansion in heaven, but wasn't ready for it yet.

She looked down and saw an old housecoat at the foot of the bed. She said to herself, "I wouldn't care a bit about discarding that old thing for a new one." The fear subsided, and she prayed, "Lord, if my old body gets in such a fix that I can't live in it, then I'm willing to say goodbye to this world."

By submitting herself to God, she won the victory. She was willing to discard that old body for a new one in the resurrection. Natural death may take that old body, but spiritual death has no power over those who know the Lord.

Although the doctors didn't expect her to live two years, by God's grace, she lived victoriously another ten. Faye never lost her smile, because she knew she has a part in the first resurrection.

> PRAYER: Dear Lord, thank you for your promise of resurrection. In the face of death, comfort me with your love, so that I can comfort others who are experiencing the same thing. Amen.

---

[a] Fifth beatitude of Revelation.

The Last Enemy 20:11–15

On Easter morning, death could not keep Jesus in the tomb. It was empty. Satan, the accuser, could not keep him in the tomb. He had never sinned. The stone covering the doorway could not keep him in the tomb. He could walk through walls. The guards could not keep him in the tomb. They fainted. The stone was rolled away by an angel so that we could see inside. The angel announced, "He has been resurrected, just as he said. Come and see the place where he lay."

The last enemy was death. Read the remainder of chapter 20 of Revelation.

Revelation 20:11–15 (HCSB)

> 11 Then I saw a great white throne and One seated on it. Earth and heaven fled from His presence, and no place was found for them. 12 I also saw the dead, the great and the small, standing before the throne, and books were opened. Another book was opened, which is the book of life, and the dead were judged according to their works by what was written in the books.
>
> 13 Then the sea gave up its dead, and Death and Hades gave up their dead; all were judged according to their works. 14 Death and Hades were thrown into the lake of fire. This is the second death, the lake of fire. 15 And anyone not found written in the book of life was thrown into the lake of fire.

Paul tells us, "The wages of sin is death."[51] This victory consists of the final accounting for those wages.

John saw a great white throne, a courtroom. It was so awesome that creation wanted to run away. Everyone was resurrected to face judgment according to what he had done during his life. This is the resurrection that Martha mentioned at Lazarus' funeral.[52] This is the judgment that Solomon expected when he wrote Ecclesiastes.[53]

Most people live from moment to moment, without concern for the eternal consequences of life's actions. TV commercials and retail merchandising try to ingrain living from one impulse to the next. "Do whatever feels good!" may sound good, but God's judgment won't be based on good feelings. It will be objective and thorough. Not only will heroic deeds and gross sin be considered, but also anonymous kindnesses, white lies in private, and the secret thoughts of the heart.[54]

Jesus is the one who will sit on the throne.[55] He is the only man qualified to be fair, objective, and thorough.

The first death is when the physical body dies. The lake of fire is called the *second death*. We have already seen the Beast, the False Prophet, and Sa-

---

[51] Romans 6:23 (KJV).
[52] John 11:24.
[53] Ecclesiastes 12:13–14.
[54] Ecclesiastes 11:9.
[55] Matthew 16:27.

tan thrown in there. The criterion for joining them was that one's name was missing from the Book of Life.

The Book of Life is mentioned throughout the Old Testament. It was simply God's list of the righteous.[56] Through the ages, a person's name was removed from the list because that person sinned.[57] Because all have sinned, one would think that the list must be empty.

However, Paul referred to Christians in Philippi as "the rest of my fellow workers, whose names are in the Book of Life."[58] A blotted out name is not inevitable. Jesus died so that we can have the righteousness of God, and thus, not have our names blotted out.[59] God promised to not blot out the names of those who repent.[60] That can include us.

> The last enemy to be abolished is death. For God has put everything under His feet.
> 1 Corinthians 15:26–27 (HCSB)

The last enemy to be deposed was death and the grave. They too were thrown into the lake of fire. Death is the result of sin. This is the final stroke of victory over sin.

Many Christians have a difficult time when a loved one dies, or even before that, when a loved one has a terminal disease. My mother was diagnosed with "terminal cancer" about ten years before she died. Even while she had generally good health, many Christian friends had difficulty talking with her about her health. They were trying to deny the reality of the cancer in her body. She tried to share with them that, for a Christian, the first death is not the end, and need not be dreaded. Even though we miss her now, it is comforting to know that we will be reunited around the throne of Jesus. Because of Jesus, we will have victory over death.

The fourth victory is the judgment of mankind and victory over death.

> When this corruptible is clothed with incorruptibility, and this mortal is clothed with immortality, then the saying that is written will take place: Death has been swallowed up in victory. Death, where is your victory? Death, where is your sting? Now the sting of death is sin, and the power of sin is the law. But thanks be to God, who gives us the victory through our Lord Jesus Christ!
> 1 Corinthians 15:54–57 (HCSB)

FOR PERSONAL STUDY
Judgment (20:11–15)

1. What would it feel like to stand before the throne of verse 11?

---
[56] Psalms 69:28.
[57] Exodus 32:32–33.
[58] Philippians 4:3 (NIV).
[59] Romans 3:22.
[60] 3:5.

2. What is the difference between the way the Book of Life and the "other books" are used?

3. Why is your name in the Book of Life?

4. Who is defeated in this passage?

5. How would it feel to face death without your name in the Book of Life? ... to face the death of a loved one?

6. When facing death, what difference would it make to know your name is in the Book of Life?

The Liberation of Creation

The real estate agent showed us through the house, hoping we would rent it. At the end of the hall was a tiny bedroom, painted light blue. The white clouds on the walls and colors around the door frame told us that a little person had been the previous resident. Painting the room like the sky reminded the little one of the love and comfort of Mom and Dad. The rainbow in the sky reminds us that God promised not to destroy the land again with a flood. The rainbow also reminds us that He promised to judge the Earth with fire, and to create a new home for everyone who is in Christ.

> God gave Noah the rainbow sign,
> No more water, but fire next time.
> You better get a home in that rock,
> Don't you see.
>
> Traditional Spiritual

Read this section's Scripture passage.

Revelation 21:1–8 (HCSB)

---

1 Then I saw a new heaven and a new earth, for the first heaven and the first earth had passed away, and the sea no longer existed. 2 I also saw the Holy City, new Jerusalem, coming down out of heaven from God, prepared like a bride adorned for her husband.
  3 Then I heard a loud voice from the throne:

> Look! God's dwelling is with humanity,
> and He will live with them.
> They will be His people,
> and God Himself will be with them
> and be their God.
> 4 He will wipe away every tear from their eyes.
> Death will no longer exist;
> grief, crying, and pain will exist no longer,
> because the previous things have passed away.

> 5 Then the One seated on the throne said, "Look! I am making everything new." He also said, "Write, because these words are faithful and true." 6 And He said to me, "It is done! I am the Alpha and the Omega, the Beginning and the End. I will give water as a gift to the thirsty from the spring of life. 7 The victor will inherit these things, and I will be his God, and he will be My son. 8 But the cowards, unbelievers, vile, murderers, sexually immoral, sorcerers, idolaters, and all liars—their share will be in the lake that burns with fire and sulfur, which is the second death."

Many prophetic Scriptures mention the Day of the Lord, or a similar phrase. Peter explained that the destruction of the old Earth will be a part of the Day of the Lord, so that God can provide a new home for us.[61] Peter said that the old order will be destroyed by fire and heat. Through the centuries, this seemed fantastic. Now that science has learned of the atomic bomb, the hydrogen bomb, and the explosion of stars and galaxies, it seems like a natural way for the universe to end. For us who believe, it will be only the beginning.

As we saw in chapter 1 of Revelation, Jesus is the Alpha and the Omega. He is not limited by time.[62] He promises eternal life to whoever will receive it. He is offering to make us his children. But those who rebel against him have their place too, the lake of fire.[63]

The new heaven and new Earth will be a place where we will have an intimate relationship with God, like a bride and her husband. It will be a place of joy and delights, as Isaiah prophesied.

> For I will create a new heaven and a new earth; the past events will not be remembered or come to mind. Then be glad and rejoice forever in what I am creating; for I will create Jerusalem to be a joy and its people to be a delight. I will rejoice in Jerusalem and be glad in My people. The sound of weeping and crying will no longer be heard in her.
>
> Isaiah 65:17–19 (HCSB)

The fifth victory is the creation of a new heaven and a new Earth.

FOR PERSONAL STUDY
A New Heaven and New Earth (21:1–8)

1. List characteristics of the new creation mentioned in the passage, and then list corresponding characteristics of creation today.

2. Who will live on the new Earth? Who will not?

---
[61] 2 Peter 3:10–13.
[62] 1:8.
[63] Isaiah 66:22–24.

3. How close does God want to be to His people?

4. What helps you get closer to God?

The City of God

In my neighborhood, there are crowds of people, bustling traffic, housing developments, shopping centers, playgrounds, and parks. This place has grown so quickly that it has city life, even though the city limits are a few miles east of here. Rather than expand the old, the neighbors are talking about making this area a new city. It will have its own streetlights, courtroom, and mayor.

God is planning a new city, too. Read the remainder of chapter 21.

Revelation 21:9–27 (HCSB)

> 9 Then one of the seven angels, who had held the seven bowls filled with the seven last plagues, came and spoke with me: "Come, I will show you the bride, the wife of the Lamb." 10 He then carried me away in the Spirit to a great and high mountain and showed me the holy city, Jerusalem, coming down out of heaven from God, 11 arrayed with God's glory. Her radiance was like a very precious stone, like a jasper stone, bright as crystal. 12 The city had a massive high wall, with 12 gates. Twelve angels were at the gates; the names of the 12 tribes of Israel's sons were inscribed on the gates. 13 There were three gates on the east, three gates on the north, three gates on the south, and three gates on the west. 14 The city wall had 12 foundations, and the 12 names of the Lamb's 12 apostles were on the foundations.
>
> 15 The one who spoke with me had a gold measuring rod to measure the city, its gates, and its wall. 16 The city is laid out in a square; its length and width are the same. He measured the city with the rod at 12,000 stadia. Its length, width, and height are equal. 17 Then he measured its wall, 144 cubits according to human measurement, which the angel used. 18 The building material of its wall was jasper, and the city was pure gold like clear glass.
>
> 19 The foundations of the city wall were adorned with every kind of precious stone:
>
>> the first foundation jasper,
>> the second sapphire,
>> the third chalcedony,
>> the fourth emerald,
>> 20 the fifth sardonyx,
>> the sixth carnelian,
>> the seventh chrysolite,
>> the eighth beryl,

> the ninth topaz,
> the tenth chrysoprase,
> the eleventh jacinth,
> the twelfth amethyst.
>
> 21 The 12 gates are 12 pearls; each individual gate was made of a single pearl. The broad street of the city was pure gold, like transparent glass.
>
> 22 I did not see a sanctuary in it, because the Lord God the Almighty and the Lamb are its sanctuary. 23 The city does not need the sun or the moon to shine on it, because God's glory illuminates it, and its lamp is the Lamb. 24 The nations will walk in its light, and the kings of the earth will bring their glory into it. 25 Each day its gates will never close because it will never be night there. 26 They will bring the glory and honor of the nations into it. 27 Nothing profane will ever enter it: no one who does what is vile or false, but only those written in the Lamb's book of life.

Our friends are from all over the country. If you had listened closely at the dinner table at our house a few weeks ago, you might have distinguished accents from Arkansas, Indiana, Minnesota, New York, Texas, and even Germany. Like an accent, our lives give us away. We can't hide the fact that we don't really belong here. Like Abraham, we can be citizens of the new Jerusalem, even though we are temporarily living in a fallen world.[64]

God has a new city in mind. Jesus will be the mayor. The next victory gives us more detail about the bride of Christ, all believers, the church. She was compared to a city, the new Jerusalem.[65]

This glorious city contrasts with Babylon, Satan's counterfeit city. This city was full of life. Babylon was full of the blood of martyrs. This city was pure and clean. Babylon was corrupt and filthy. Our lives indicate where we feel at home—in the new Jerusalem or in Babylon. "Home is where the heart is."

Let us consider the detailed description of the new Jerusalem, and look for insight into the character of the victorious church. John saw the city coming down from heaven. The church was created by God, through the blood of Jesus. It was shining with the glory of God, like a brilliant jewel. Similarly, we should be reflecting the glory of God in our lives day to day. It had twelve gates, the twelve tribes of Israel. The gate in ancient times was the city courtroom. Through Israel, God gave the law to mankind. Also, a gate is an entrance to the city. Through Israel, God sent His Son into the world to be the door for us.[66] It had twelve foundation stones, the twelve apostles. Starting with the apostles, the church spread around the world. The city was big in every direction. There is room for all God's people.

---

[64] Hebrews 11:9–10.
[65] 21:2.
[66] John 10:7–9.

The walls were thick enough to clearly define the boundaries of the city. Today, it is hard to see where a major city begins and ends, because of surrounding suburbs. Similarly, it is often hard to tell the difference between a denomination and a cult. In that day, it will be easy to see the boundaries of the church, those whose names are in the Book of Life.

There are Christian groups which hold a doctrine that only members of their group will be saved. Won't they be surprised when the rest of us show up? Membership in a cult won't shut one out. Membership in the best church in town won't guarantee entrance. I know people involved in cults who have a simple sincere faith in Jesus. We might as well get used to spending time with believers from different styles, traditions, and cultures. Paul warned the Corinthians not to let divisions and strife interfere with spreading the gospel, because that is the job we have in common.[67]

The city was made of precious and beautiful materials. For example, each foundation was made of a different kind of precious stone. Similarly, there were twelve precious stones on the breastplate of the high priest in Moses' tabernacle,[68] depicting how precious the tribes of Israel are to the Lord. We, the church, are precious to the Lord.

There are certain things that do not belong in the new Jerusalem. There is no special place to meet God. He lives inside us. There is no night, no sun, and no moon. The glory of God always lights the city. Similarly, our lives will be lighted as we follow him.[69]

There is nothing unclean in the city. The Old Testament designated certain foods and certain aspects of daily life as clean and unclean. This distinction was a practical reminder of God's holiness and his sinlessness. The only ones who will come into the city are those who have been washed in the blood of the Lamb, those whose names are in the Book of Life. You can't get in by joining an organization. It takes a personal relationship with Jesus to become clean.

The sixth victory is the church becoming the Bride of Christ, a holy city.

FOR PERSONAL STUDY
The New Jerusalem   (21:9–27)

1. List the new Jerusalem's characteristics?

2. On your list, check characteristics that illustrate God's care for his people. Which are your favorites? Why?

3. What kind of overall feeling do you get from the description of the new Jerusalem?

---

[67] 1 Corinthians 1:11–13 and 1 Corinthians 3:3–9.
[68] Exodus 28:15–21.
[69] John 8:12.

Down by the Riverside

California's San Joaquin valley has orchards that stretch for miles. Without irrigation from the river, the valley becomes an arid desert, but when watered, it produces fruit for grocery stores across the nation.

God, too, has an orchard irrigated by a river. Read this section's scripture passage.

Revelation 22:1–5 (HCSB)

---

1 Then he showed me the river of living water, sparkling like crystal, flowing from the throne of God and of the Lamb 2 down the middle of the broad street of the city. The tree of life was on both sides of the river, bearing 12 kinds of fruit, producing its fruit every month. The leaves of the tree are for healing the nations, 3 and there will no longer be any curse. The throne of God and of the Lamb will be in the city, and His slaves will serve Him. 4 They will see His face, and His name will be on their foreheads. 5 Night will no longer exist, and people will not need lamplight or sunlight, because the Lord God will give them light. And they will reign forever and ever.

Through the middle of the city ran a river with the water of life. Jesus is the source of the water of life for us, too.

The woman of Samaria was probably hot and thirsty when she went to the well. When Jesus offered her the water of life, she thought it would be like a kitchen sink. Later, she realized that Jesus was offering eternal life, which is even better.[70]

This river described in Revelation had the tree of life on either side. When Adam and Eve sinned, they were not allowed to eat from the tree of life, and the ground was cursed.[71] In the new Jerusalem, the tree of life will be freely available.

The throne of God was in the city. He was accessible. His servants were marked with His name. We are already marked as belonging to God by the Holy Spirit in us.

The city of God is eternal. We may be living in temporary places now, but we are looking forward to that eternal city.[72]

If we draw nourishment from God's Spirit, and let spiritual fruit grow in our lives, we can be a tree of life to those around us. Paul listed nine kinds of fruit of the Spirit. "But the fruit of the Spirit is love, joy, peace, patience, kindness, goodness, faithfulness, gentleness, self-control; against such things there is no law."[73]

---

[70] John 4:13–14.
[71] Genesis 3:17–19,24.
[72] Hebrews 11:10.
[73] Galatians 5:22–23 (NASB).

> The man who trusts in the Lord, whose confidence indeed is the Lord, is blessed. He will be like a tree planted by water: it sends its roots out toward a stream, it doesn't fear when heat comes, and its foliage remains green. It will not worry in a year of drought or cease producing fruit.
>
> Jeremiah 17:7–8 (HCSB)

The seventh victory is God's living water producing abundant fruit.

FOR PERSONAL STUDY
The River of Life   (22:1–5)

1. List aspects of living along the river of life.

2. List the fruits in Galatians 5:22–23.

3. Which items on your two lists can you start practicing now?

Review

The American home-town football team won the championship. They had perfected each aspect of the game: passing, running, blocking, defense, and special situations. The quarterback would throw to his receivers just out of reach of the other side. The line blocked anyone from touching the guy running with the ball. The defense wouldn't let the other side move ahead. The kicker could put the ball between the goal posts. Each contributed to the ultimate victory.

Christ's ultimate victory also has several aspects, seen in chapter 17 through 22:5. The flow of visions can be outlined into seven visions which, as a whole, depict his complete victory.

1. The world system will be destroyed.

2. Satan's agents of oppression and deception will be defeated.

3. Satan, the deceiver, will be bound and then defeated.

4. Mankind will be judged, and death will be defeated.

5. The old creation will pass away and God will provide a new heaven and a new Earth.

6. The church will be the Bride of Christ, a holy city.

7. God's living water will produce abundant fruit.

In the first four visions, Christ's enemies were defeated. The last three visions balance the picture by revealing good things that are part of eternal life. When Jesus returns, he will clean up the mess that Satan and his followers have made. Death, the last enemy, will be defeated, too. The old corrupt system will be replaced with a new creation, community, and life.

Even though eternity seems a long way off, knowing about the ultimate victory equips us for everyday life. Our goal is to live victoriously today. These visions give us insights, such as these. Do not rely on this world system for security. Resist Satan's agents of oppression and deception. Do not be deceived by Satan. Live righteously, mindful of the judgment, and do not be afraid of death. Be thankful for this creation and look forward to the next. Be devoted to Jesus, as a bride is devoted to her beloved. Cultivate the fruits of the Spirit.

We may have spiritual battles from time to time. The forces of evil may seem overwhelming. Problems may be intimidating. But by obeying these Scriptures, victorious living can be ours. After all, Jesus wins.

FOR PERSONAL STUDY
Review—Seven-Fold Victory   (17:1–22:5)

1. What is the most important victory in each passage?

2. What has been Satan's plan at each of these times:
   - In the Fall?
   - In Old Testament history?
   - In the crucifixion?
   - In modern history?
   - In the events of Revelation 12 and 13?
   - In the events of Revelation 17–20?

3. How has God defeated Satan's efforts at each of these times?

4. List ways God cares for you?

5. List the passages from chapters 17–22 that are worshipful. Picture yourself in each worship scene and meditate on it.

Conclusion

Reservations Suggested

> Blessed are those who wash their robes, that they may have the right to the tree of life, and may enter by the gates into the city.[a]
>
> Revelation 22:14 (NASB)

"Reservations Suggested." "Jacket Required." I was browsing through the phone-book advertisements looking for a place to eat. The ad said, "A Four-Star Rating," and "The food and service are world renowned." I thought, "This must be an elegant place, but it's probably expensive." Then I concluded, "Well, it's worth the cost when its for someone you love."

God has a restaurant, too. It's located just inside the city limits. We have robes of righteousness to wear, washed in Jesus' blood. The buffet has twelve kinds of fruit, and bread from heaven. The occasion is a wedding reception, and I understand that the food and service are out of this world. Jesus has already made reservations for us, and paid the bill in advance. It was worth the cost, because he loves us.

> PRAYER: Father, thank you for giving me eternal life through your Son Jesus. I'm looking forward to dining at your restaurant. Amen.

---

[a] Seventh beatitude of Revelation.

6

Conclusion

> The true light, who gives light to everyone, was coming into the world. He was in the world, and the world was created through Him, yet the world did not recognize Him. He came to His own, and His own people did not receive Him. But to all who did receive Him, He gave them the right to be children of God, to those who believe in His name, who were born, not of blood, or of the will of the flesh, or of the will of man, but of God. The Word became flesh and took up residence among us. We observed His glory, the glory as the One and Only Son from the Father, full of grace and truth.
>
> John 1:9–14 (HCSB)

When Jesus came to earth about two thousand years ago, most people did not recognize that he is God's Son. Most people still do not acknowledge him. When he came to John in a vision, his identity was obvious. When we read "the revelation of Jesus Christ,"[1] we clearly see his glory. The vision had symbols representing his character and authority. When Revelation is fulfilled, God's Son will be recognized by all.

Panorama

The Chinese pavilion at Disney's Epcot Center presents a tour of China through a movie which surrounds the audience. The aerial view of mountains and countryside is exhilarating. The sights and sounds of a crowded harbor are fascinating. To take the panorama in, all at once, is overwhelming.

We have approached Revelation as a panorama of God's purpose, which also is exhilarating, fascinating, and overwhelming. Major themes of Revelation are woven together and reappear over and over like threads of a large tapestry. Our outline of Revelation has four main sections, plus a prologue and an epilogue. Each section focuses our attention on an aspect of God's message.

---

[1] 1:1.

Section I consists of letters to seven churches. Jesus advised each one to overcome. Section II consists of the visions that followed opening each of the seals on a scroll. The vision of the seventh seal consists of visions after each of seven trumpets sounded. Despite all the groans of creation, mankind did not repent. Section III consists of seven signs which depict spiritual warfare and the forces on each side. The seventh sign consists of visions after each of seven bowls of plagues were poured out. Satan viciously attacked God's people, who steadfastly countered his onslaught. Section IV consists of seven visions which depict our victory in Christ. All of Satan's forces were defeated, and Jesus reigned supreme.

The following summarizes applications of the four main sections and discusses other threads that occur throughout Revelation.

The church must overcome. The letters to seven churches, Section I, depict local groups of Christians, with various strengths and problems. Ephesus was industrious, but lacking their first love. Smyrna was faithful, but suffering persecution. Pergamum was tolerant of false doctrine. Thyatira was tolerant of corrupt leadership. Sardis had a distinguished reputation, but was cold and dead in reality. Philadelphia was obscure but faithful. Laodicea was self confident, but lukewarm.

Each letter to the seven churches included a promise "to him who overcomes." At the end of Revelation, John saw God's seven-fold victory. Each of the seven promises at the beginning hinted of a victory at the end. Ephesus was promised to eat of the tree of life. The seventh victory described the tree of life. Smyrna was promised not to be hurt by the second death. The fourth victory was over death itself. Pergamum was promised to eat of hidden manna, and a new name. The first victory was over the Babylon, who had an abominable name, and was the source of wealth for the world's merchants. Thyatira was promised authority over the nations. The second victory was over the Beast and the False Prophet who had ruled the Earth with Satan's authority. Sardis was promised a white robe and a name in the Book of Life. The fifth victory says the Bride of Christ was "adorned for her husband." The white linen of the Bride is the righteousness of believers. Eternal judgment in the fourth victory was based on the Book of Life. Philadelphia was promised to be a pillar in the temple of God, and to be named New Jerusalem. The sixth victory described the New Jerusalem. Laodicea was promised to sit on the throne with Christ. The third victory was over Satan, and described thrones for believers, ruling the Earth with Christ for a thousand years.

We can apply each letter to local Christian groups that are similar to each church, or even to our personal lives. The advice Jesus gave each church is relevant today and the promises of victory apply to whomever will overcome.

The world must repent. The seven-sealed scroll, Section II, depicts scenes familiar in our time. Each scene of the first six seals shows us the effects of sin. The seventh seal reveals God's solution—repentance.

The visions of the first four seals were four horsemen who represented oppression, war, famine, and death from plagues. Opening the fifth seal revealed martyrs for the faith who await vindication from God. The vision of the sixth seal consisted of catastrophes in nature.

The vision of the seventh seal consisted of seven bugle calls. They are intended to get our attention. Natural disasters like those of the first six trumpets make people realize that they need to repent. The seventh trumpet announced the righteous reign of Jesus. It is God's final call to repentance. We have many modern local examples of bugle calls to repentance. The first four visions were disasters in nature, such as forest fires, seas polluted by red tide (toxic algae blooms), rivers poisoned by toxic chemicals and bacteria, and air filled with smog and volcanic ash clouds. The vision of the fifth trumpet reminds us of demonic torment today. The vision of the sixth trumpet reminds us of local deaths from volcanic eruptions. Each of these disasters makes us realize how fragile life is, and that repentance today is what God wants from mankind.

Sections II has interludes between sixth and seventh visions. Between the sixth and seventh seals, God sealed 144 thousand of his servants with a signet, and between the sixth and seventh trumpets, the gospel was preached by his witnesses. These give a closer look at God's relationship with his people.

We can apply the seven-sealed scroll to our lives by taking God's perspective on the sufferings of this world. All the Earth groans under the weight of sin. Creation, Christians, and the world's people alike feel the effects. God is hoping we will turn to him for the solution.

The devil is angry. The seven signs, Section III, depict our spiritual battle and the forces on each side. The seventh sign consists of visions after each of seven bowls of plagues were poured out. Section III also has interludes between sixth and seventh visions. Between the sixth and seventh signs, God gathered a harvest of grain representing believers, and a harvest of grapes representing God's wrath against sin. Between the sixth and seventh plagues, Satan gathered his forces for battle against the Lord.

On one side of our spiritual battle is Satan, the dragon, who hates God's people. The agents of Satan, the Beast and the False Prophet, are making war against God's people. Worldly power and religiosity are Satan's agents. Their spiritual weapons are coercion and deception.

On the other side, God has given us weapons of spiritual warfare. Unrestrained worship is a spiritual weapon. Preaching the gospel is a spiritual weapon. Recognizing that society is fallen is a spiritual weapon. Refusing to be identified with the world is a spiritual weapon. Finally, the seventh sign demonstrated that God's wrath against sin is the ultimate spiritual weapon.

When we apply the seven plagues of the seventh sign to today, they show that Satan's kingdom is bankrupt. Satan's prosperity leads to suffering. Satan's power is lifeless. Satan's life is polluted and disgusting, because of the blood of martyrs. There is no shade from the heat of God's wrath. The world's way of thinking is darkness. Borders are insecure. Most of all, God has judged sin. Even though it is obvious who is going to win this war, mankind did not repent. They cursed God over and over.

Jesus wins. The seven visions of victory, Section IV, portray the defeat of Satan and his followers and the redemption of believers.

The first four visions depict Jesus' victory over evil. The world system will be destroyed. Satan's agents of oppression and deception will be defeated. Satan himself, the deceiver, will be bound and then defeated. Mankind will be judged, and death will be defeated.

The last three visions depict what God is planning for the redeemed. The old creation will pass away and God will provide a new heaven and a new Earth. The church will be the Bride of Christ, a holy city. God's living water will produce abundant fruit. Christ's victory will be complete.

Worship. Worship is a thread of the tapestry. Scenes of worship in heaven appear throughout Revelation. As we read, we can join our hearts with the heavenly throng, letting our worship mirror theirs. The first chapter describes who God is, what he has done for us, and attributes of the risen Christ.[2] The fourth chapter describes the throne of God. Those around the throne worshiped him because he is holy and he is the creator of all things.[3] We see in the fifth chapter that Jesus, the Lamb of God, is worthy of our praise.[4] In the seventh chapter, those who have been faithful through persecution worshiped Jesus, because he cares for them.[5] We see in chapter eleven the throng around God's throne giving thanks because Jesus has begun to reign.[6] Heaven rejoiced in chapter twelve, because Satan was cast out of heaven.[7] In chapter fifteen, those who had overcome Satan's agents worshiped the Lord.[8] In chapter nineteen, the multitude in heaven rejoiced over the fall of Babylon.[9] All of these passages are opportunities for us to worship the Lord and to echo the message of those in heaven.

Repentance. Repentance is a thread of the tapestry. The call to repentance and the world's response is heard over and over in Revelation. The churches at Ephesus, Pergamum, Sardis, and Laodicea were called to repent.[10] After six trumpets had sounded the world's people did not repent.[11] After the fourth bowl of plagues was poured out and again after the fifth bowl of plagues the

---

[2] 1:1–8 and 1:9–20.
[3] 4:1–11.
[4] 5:1–14.
[5] 7:9–17.
[6] 11:15–19.
[7] 12:10–12.
[8] 15:3–4.
[9] 19:1–8.
[10] 2:5, 2:16, 3:3, and 3:19.
[11] 9:20–21.

world's people did not repent.[12] After receiving a bitter-sweet book, John was told he must prophesy; his message must have included the call to repentance.[13] The two witnesses prophesied against the world's people; their message also must have included the call to repentance.[14] The fourth sign announced the gospel, which includes the call to repentance.[15] These passages emphasize that the Lord wants mankind to repent. He offers mercy and new life, if one will recognize sin for what it is and turn away from it.

Sealed. Being sealed by the Holy Spirit is a thread of the tapestry. When we read about believers being sealed with a signet, we can apply this to the way the Holy Spirit is a seal on our hearts.[16] During the interlude between the sixth and seventh seals, the Lord sealed 144,000 from the tribes of Israel.[17] In the vision of the fifth trumpet, the sealed ones were protected.[18] In the third sign, the 144,000 worshiped the Lord.[19] In the new Jerusalem, believers had the Lord's name on their foreheads, showing that they belong to him.[20] The Holy Spirit in our lives is a constant reminder of who we belong to. We belong to Jesus.

Faithful. Another thread of the tapestry is the faithfulness of Jesus and the call for us to be faithful. From the very start of Revelation, Jesus is identified as the faithful witness.[21] At the end of Revelation, we realize that the words of Jesus are faithful and true.[22] Jesus knows when his followers are faithful. He told Smyrna to be faithful even unto death.[23] In Pergamum, Antipas was a faithful witness.[24] Jesus knew about the faithfulness of the church in Thyatira.[25] When Jesus comes again, faithful ones will accompany him.[26] I want to be among those who are with Jesus on that day.

Martyrs. Martyrs are a thread of the tapestry. Some Christians find themselves confronted with a choice: deny their Lord or be killed. In Pergamum, Antipas was a martyr.[27] In the vision of the fifth seal, martyrs were under the

---

[12] 16:9,11.
[13] 10:10–11.
[14] 11:3.
[15] 14:6–7.
[16] Ephesians 1:13–14.
[17] 7:3–8.
[18] 9:4.
[19] 14:1–5.
[20] 22:4.
[21] 1:5, 3:14, and 19:11.
[22] 21:5 and 22:6.
[23] 2:10.
[24] 2:13.
[25] 2:19.
[26] 17:14.
[27] 2:13.

altar awaiting their vindication.[28] In the interlude between the sixth and seventh trumpets, God's two witnesses were martyred and resurrected.[29] Killing faithful believers is one of Satan's tactics in our spiritual war. The False Prophet was permitted to martyr those who did not worship the Beast.[30] The prostitute city of Babylon was drunk on the blood of believers.[31] But death cannot stop Jesus' victory. We saw that resurrected martyrs reigned with Jesus in the millennium.[32] God will vindicate those who have been killed for being faithful.

Judgment. Judgment of sin is another thread of the tapestry. God will clean up the mess that sin has wreaked. In the vision of the fifth seal, martyrs called for judgment.[33] In the interlude between the sixth and seventh trumpets, the two witnesses announced God's judgment on sin.[34] The seventh trumpet announced that the time for judgment had arrived.[35] In the vision of the fourth sign, the angel with the gospel announced that the time for judgment had arrived.[36] After the third bowl of plagues, a voice from the altar said God's judgments are righteous.[37] The prostitute city of Babylon was judged.[38] In the vision of the great white throne, the dead were judged for what they had done.[39] Jesus is the one who will judge.[40]

Jesus reigns. Jesus will reign over Planet Earth is a thread of the tapestry. At the beginning of Revelation, Jesus is identified as the ruler of the kings of the Earth.[41] The seventh trumpet announced Jesus will reign.[42] After the fall of Babylon, there was rejoicing because the Jesus had begun to reign.[43] Jesus will reign during the millennium.[44] All will submit to Jesus whether they like it or not, because Jesus will rule the nations with a rod (scepter) of iron.[45]

Panorama. The threads of Revelation are fascinating to examine individually, but the majestic pattern of the tapestry comes into focus as we step back to see the major themes. The church must overcome. The world must repent. The devil is angry. Jesus wins.

---

[28] 6:9–11.
[29] 11:7–10.
[30] 13:15.
[31] 17:6, 18:24, and 19:2.
[32] 20:4.
[33] 6:10.
[34] 11:10.
[35] 11:18.
[36] 14:7.
[37] 16:7.
[38] 17:1, 18:8, 18:10, 18:20, and 19:2.
[39] 20:12–13.
[40] 19:11.
[41] 1:5.
[42] 11:15.
[43] 19:6.
[44] 20:4, 6.
[45] 2:27, 12:5, and 19:15.

FOR PERSONAL STUDY
Revelation as a Whole

1. Review the main ideas of each section.
   - I. Letters to seven churches (1:9–3:22).
   - II. The seven-sealed scroll (4:1–11:19).
   - III. Seven signs (12:1–16:21).
   - IV. Seven-fold victory (17:1–22:5).
   - Prologue and Epilogue (1:1–8, 22:6–21).

2. What have we learned concerning:
   - God's relationship with His people?
   - God's justice and judgment?
   - The character and roles of Jesus?

Come, Lord Jesus

The title of this book of the Bible is "The revelation of Jesus Christ." Jesus is revealing something urgent to us.

Read the remainder of chapter 22 of Revelation.

Revelation 22:6–21 (HCSB)

---

6 Then he said to me, "These words are faithful and true. And the Lord, the God of the spirits of the prophets, has sent His angel to show His slaves what must quickly take place."

7 "Look, I am coming quickly! The one who keeps the prophetic words of this book is blessed."

8 I, John, am the one who heard and saw these things. When I heard and saw them, I fell down to worship at the feet of the angel who had shown them to me. 9 But he said to me, "Don't do that! I am a fellow slave with you, your brothers the prophets, and those who keep the words of this book. Worship God." 10 He also said to me, "Don't seal the prophetic words of this book, because the time is near. 11 Let the unrighteous go on in unrighteousness; let the filthy go on being made filthy; let the righteous go on in righteousness; and let the holy go on being made holy."

12 "Look! I am coming quickly, and My reward is with Me to repay each person according to what he has done. 13 I am the Alpha and the Omega, the First and the Last, the Beginning and the End.

14 "Blessed are those who wash their robes, so that they may have the right to the tree of life and may enter the city by the gates. 15 Outside are the dogs, the sorcerers, the sexually immoral, the

> murderers, the idolaters, and everyone who loves and practices lying.
>
> 16 "I, Jesus, have sent My angel to attest these things to you for the churches. I am the Root and the Offspring of David, the Bright Morning Star."
>
> 17 Both the Spirit and the bride say, "Come!" Anyone who hears should say, "Come!" And the one who is thirsty should come. Whoever desires should take the living water as a gift.
>
> 18 I testify to everyone who hears the prophetic words of this book: If anyone adds to them, God will add to him the plagues that are written in this book. 19 And if anyone takes away from the words of this prophetic book, God will take away his share of the tree of life and the holy city, written in this book.
>
> 20 He who testifies about these things says, "Yes, I am coming quickly."
>
> Amen! Come, Lord Jesus!
>
> 21 The grace of the Lord Jesus be with all the saints. Amen.

John carefully wrote down what he saw and heard. We can understand it and put its teaching into practice. If we are preoccupied by symbols, charts, and diagrams, we risk falling into the trap of worshiping the message of Revelation, rather than the author, God himself.

Many passages in Revelation draw us into times of meditation and worship. When we read about the scene around the throne, our spirits join the creatures and elders in worship. Let us take time for worship as we read Revelation again and again.

God told Daniel to seal up his prophesy until the end-time.[46] Some suppose that God makes all prophesy mysterious and hard to understand. This is not true of Revelation. It is not a mystery for experts to unravel. God told John not to seal up the prophesy, because Jesus is coming again soon.

When Jesus does come, he will judge and reward everyone according to what they have done. Those who have been cleansed from sin will live with him forever. Outside will be those who continued in sins, such as the occult, immorality, murder, idolatry, and deception.

His invitation to life is open. The water of life is available to anyone who will repent from sin and receive it.

Some are tempted to supplement God's Word with speculations. This is frequently excused as "interpretation," even though the connection to the text is just an isolated word or phrase. It is important to be clear-minded, distinguishing a basic timeless interpretation from personal application and speculation. We must be careful not to ascribe Scriptural authority to human ideas.

For others, it is tempting to act as though Revelation is not part of God's Word. "It's so hard to understand." "Maybe it will go away, if I ignore it." The

---

[46] Daniel 12:4,9–10.

effort to understand and apply it will pay off richly. It is part of God's Word and it will feed our souls.

Don't try to elaborate on God's Word. It is complete. Don't try to minimize what God has said. It applies to us.

Overcoming is difficult. Along with creation, we groan because of the effects of sin. Spiritual warfare is real and demands sacrifices. Following Jesus is not easy now, but the victory in him will be sweet.

> He who testifies about these things says, "Yes, I am coming quickly." Amen! Come, Lord Jesus!
>
> Revelation 22:20 (HCSB)

FOR PERSONAL STUDY
Epilogue (22:6–21)

1. What is the primary message from Jesus in verses 6–13?

2. What is the main idea of verses 14–17?

3. How does this passage contribute to the overall impact of the rest of Revelation?

APPENDIX

For Group Study

This appendix can be used as a discussion guide by a group studying Revelation. The FOR PERSONAL STUDY questions throughout the book may be used for group discussion. Their purpose is to help you discover the main ideas of Revelation. Because Revelation is rather long, and filled with rich imagery, a group study will require commitment and dedication. The primary objective should be to gain an overview, and to apply what you learn to your life.

A very important aspect of a group Bible study is sharing with each other. To cultivate this, be open and accepting to whatever each member has to contribute. The Holy Spirit is not limited to Bible experts for teachers. He wants to use the contribution of each member of your group, young and old, new and mature Christians. The only way to benefit from each other is to truly listen to each other.

Many discussions of Revelation stray into other topics. However, most groups have only a limited amount of time. To make the best use of your time, commit yourselves to find the main ideas of the passage first. Focus on the most important lesson of the passage, leaving interesting, but less practical, details for another time.

A free open discussion must guarantee everyone the opportunity to share. The leader should guard against anyone (including himself) dominating the discussion with his own interpretation, even if that person has many good ideas. Encourage the participation of everyone.

There will be differing interpretations in your group. These can be a source of friction and hate, or occasions for love and mutual growth. Disagreements can stem from several sources. Sometimes we just use different words to say the same thing. This is overcome by listening, and by forgiving a brother when he doesn't say what he means. Sometimes we build an interpretation on a few key words, as if Revelation were a code book. Reading several translations can free us from particular words to see the main ideas. Sometimes we base our interpretation of details on other scriptures. Someone else may not relate the two passages in the same way. Sometimes we simply differ in emphasis, and sometimes we apply it differently to our lives.

For Group Study

Differing interpretations should not be a problem in your group. Some disagreements evaporate after a little discussion. Some are honest differences of opinion. All can be occasions for showing love toward each other. Too many churches have been split over interpretations of Revelation. The leader and the group should cultivate brotherly love. A "correct" interpretation of Revelation, without love, is worthless.

> And though I have the gift of prophesy, and understand all mysteries, and all knowledge, ... and have not love, I am nothing.
> 1 Corinthians 13:2 (KJV)

Four plans for group study are presented below, which range from twenty-two to six sessions, and from no homework to several hours per session. During your getting-started session, make sure each member understands the plan you have chosen.

The group studies are based on the questions FOR PERSONAL STUDY. Under each plan, a typical group session will be 45 minutes to one hour of discussion. Your may want to set aside additional time for worship and personal sharing at each session.

No-Homework Plan

- 22 sessions.

- No homework required.

- Each session consists of reading the passage and discussing the questions FOR PERSONAL STUDY.

No-Homework Plan

Session	Discussion	Reference	Page
1	Prologue	1:1–8	4
Letters to Seven Churches			
2	Among the Lampstands	1:9–20	14
	Ephesus	2:1–7	16
3	Smyrna	2:8–11	18
	Pergamum	2:12–17	20
4	Thyatira	2:18–29	24
	Sardis	3:1–6	27
5	Philadelphia	3:7–13	30
	Laodicea	3:14–22	31
6	Review	1:9–3:22	33
A Scroll with Seven Seals			
7	The Throne of God	4:1–5:14	41
8	Six Seals	6:1–17	49
	Servants of God	7:1–17	53

In-Depth Plan

No-Homework Plan (continued)

Session	Discussion	Reference	Page
The Seventh Seal—Seven Trumpets			
9	Incense	8:1–5	56
	Six Trumpets	8:6–9:21	61
	The Seventh Trumpet	11:14–19	72
10	My Witnesses	10:1–11:13	69
11	Review	4:1–11:19	75
Seven Signs			
12	The Dragon	12:1–17	85
	Beasts	12:18–13:18	91
13	A New Song	14:1–5	94
	Three Angels	14:6–13	97
14	Reapings	14:14–20	99
The Seventh Sign—Seven Bowls			
(14)	Songs	15:1–8	103
15	Six Bowls	16:1–12	107
	Three Frogs	16:13–16	108
	The Seventh Bowl	16:17–21	111
16	Review	12:1–16:21	113
Seven-Fold Victory			
17	The Fall of Babylon	17:1–19:10	127
18	Beasts Defeated	19:11–21	130
	The Dragon Bound	20:1–10	135
19	Judgment	20:11–15	138
	A New Heaven and New Earth	21:1–8	140
20	The New Jerusalem	21:9–27	143
	The River of Life	22:1–5	145
21	Review	17:1–22:5	146
22	Revelation as a Whole		155
	Epilogue	22:6–21	157

In-Depth Plan

- 14 sessions.

- About 1 hour of homework per session is required.

- The FOR PERSONAL STUDY questions will be done as homework.

The first group session will get the study started. Each subsequent group session will consist of discussing the homework, or the REVIEW questions at the end of major sections. Since everyone should be familiar with the passage, the pace should be about twice as fast as the NO HOMEWORK PLAN.

For Group Study

In-Depth Plan

Session	Discussion	Reference	Page
1	Prologue	1:1–8	4
Homework	**Letters to Seven Churches**		
	Among the Lampstands	1:9–20	14
	Ephesus	2:1–7	16
	Smyrna	2:8–11	18
	Pergamum	2:12–17	20
2	Discuss homework	1:9–2:17	
Homework	**Letters to Seven Churches (continued)**		
	Thyatira	2:18–29	24
	Sardis	3:1–6	27
	Philadelphia	3:7–13	30
	Laodicea	3:14–22	31
3	Discuss homework	2:18–3:22	
Homework	**Letters to Seven Churches (continued)**		
	Review previous homework	1:9–3:22	
4	Review	1:9–3:22	33
Homework	**A Scroll with Seven Seals**		
	The Throne of God	4:1–5:14	41
	Six Seals	6:1–17	49
	Servants of God	7:1–17	53
5	Discuss homework	4:1–7:17	
Homework	**The Seventh Seal—Seven Trumpets**		
	Incense	8:1–5	56
	Six Trumpets	8:6–9:21	61
	My Witnesses	10:1–11:13	69
	The Seventh Trumpet	11:14–19	72
6	Discuss homework	8:1–11:19	
Homework	**Seven Seals (continued)**		
	Review previous homework	4:1–11:19	
7	Review	4:1–11:19	75
Homework	**Seven Signs**		
	The Dragon	12:1–17	85
	Beasts	12:18–13:18	91
	A New Song	14:1–5	94
	Three Angels	14:6–13	97
	Reapings	14:14–20	99
8	Discuss homework	12:1–14:20	
Homework	**The Seventh Sign—Seven Bowls**		
	Songs	15:1–8	103
	Six Bowls	16:1–12	107
	Three Frogs	16:13–16	108
	The Seventh Bowl	16:17–21	111
9	Discuss homework	15:1–16:21	
Homework	**Seven Signs (continued)**		
	Review previous homework	12:1–16:21	
10	Review	12:1–16:21	113

In-Depth Plan (continued)

Session	Discussion	Reference	Page
Homework	**Seven-Fold Victory**		
	The Fall of Babylon	17:1–19:10	127
	Beasts Defeated	19:11–21	130
	The Dragon Bound	20:1–10	135
11	Discuss homework	17:1–20:10	
Homework	**Seven-Fold Victory (continued)**		
	Judgment	20:11–15	138
	A New Heaven and New Earth	21:1–8	140
	The New Jerusalem	21:9–27	143
	The River of Life	22:1–5	145
12	Discuss homework	20:11–22:5	
Homework	**Seven-Fold Victory (continued)**		
	Review previous homework	17:1–22:5	
13	Review	17:1–22:5	146
Homework	**Revelation as a Whole**		
	Review all previous homework	1:1–22:5	
	Epilogue	22:6–21	157
14	Revelation as a Whole		155

Overview Plan

- 10 sessions.

- About 1 hour of homework per session is required.

- The FOR PERSONAL STUDY questions will be done as homework.

The first group session will get the study started. Each subsequent group session will consist of discussing the REVIEW questions at the end of major sections, or an extra PERSONAL STUDY. Since this plan does not review the homework in detail, the pace should be faster than the IN DEPTH PLAN.

Overview Plan

Session	Discussion	Reference	Page
1	Prologue	1:1–8	4
Homework	**Letters to Seven Churches**		
	Among the Lampstands	1:9–20	14
	Ephesus	2:1–7	16
	Smyrna	2:8–11	18
	Pergamum	2:12–17	20
2	The Church	John 15:9–17	21

For Group Study

Overview Plan (continued)

Session	Discussion	Reference	Page
Homework	**Letters to Seven Churches (continued)**		
	Thyatira	2:18–29	24
	Sardis	3:1–6	27
	Philadelphia	3:7–13	30
	Laodicea	3:14–22	31
3	Review	1:9–3:22	33
Homework	**A Scroll with Seven Seals**		
	The Throne of God	4:1–5:14	41
	Six Seals	6:1–17	49
	Servants of God	7:1–17	53
4	The Lamb	Isaiah 52:14–53:12	43
Homework	**The Seventh Seal—Seven Trumpets**		
	Incense	8:1–5	56
	Six Trumpets	8:6–9:21	61
	My Witnesses	10:1–11:13	69
	The Seventh Trumpet	11:14–19	72
5	Review	4:1–11:19	75
Homework	**Seven Signs**		
	The Dragon	12:1–17	85
	Beasts	12:18–13:18	91
	A New Song	14:1–5	94
	Three Angels	14:6–13	97
	Reapings	14:14–20	99
6	Armor	Ephesians 6:10-20	97
Homework	**The Seventh Sign—Seven Bowls**		
	Songs	15:1–8	103
	Six Bowls	16:1–12	107
	Three Frogs	16:13–16	108
	The Seventh Bowl	16:17–21	111
7	Review	12:1–16:21	113
Homework	**Seven-Fold Victory**		
	The Fall of Babylon	17:1–19:10	127
	Beasts Defeated	19:11–21	130
	Dragon Bound	20:1–10	135
8	Washing Feet	John 13:1-16	131
Homework	**Seven-Fold Victory (continued)**		
	Judgment	20:11–15	138
	A New Heaven and New Earth	21:1–8	140
	The New Jerusalem	21:9–27	143
	The River of Life	22:1–5	145
9	Review	17:1–22:5	146
Homework	**Revelation as a Whole**		
	Review all previous homework	1:1–22:5	
	Epilogue	22:6–21	157
10	Revelation as a Whole		155

Quick Overview Plan

Quick Overview Plan

- 6 sessions.

- About 2 hours of homework per session is required.

- The FOR PERSONAL STUDY questions will be done as homework.

The first group session will get the study started. Each subsequent group session will consist of discussing the REVIEW questions at the end of major sections. Since this plan has more homework, the pace should be faster than the OVERVIEW PLAN.

Quick Overview Plan

Session	Discussion	Reference	Page
1	Prologue	1:1–8	4
Homework	**Letters to Seven Churches**		
	Among the Lampstands	1:9–20	14
	Ephesus	2:1–7	16
	Smyrna	2:8–11	18
	Pergamum	2:12–17	20
	Thyatira	2:18–29	24
	Sardis	3:1–6	27
	Philadelphia	3:7–13	30
	Laodicea	3:14–22	31
2	Review	1:9–3:22	33
Homework	**A Scroll with Seven Seals**		
	The Throne of God	4:1–5:14	41
	Six Seals	6:1–17	49
	Servants of God	7:1–17	53
	The Seventh Seal—Seven Trumpets		
	Incense	8:1–5	56
	Six Trumpets	8:6–9:21	61
	My Witnesses	10:1–11:13	69
	The Seventh Trumpet	11:14–19	72
3	Review	4:1–11:19	75
Homework	**Seven Signs**		
	The Dragon	12:1–17	85
	Beasts	12:18–13:18	91
	A New Song	14:1–5	94
	Three Angels	14:6–13	97
	Reapings	14:14–20	99
	The Seventh Sign—Seven Bowls		
	Songs	15:1–8	103
	Six Bowls	16:1–12	107
	Three Frogs	16:13–16	108
	The Seventh Bowl	16:17–21	111
4	Review	12:1–16:21	113

Quick Overview Plan (continued)

Session	Discussion	Reference	Page
Homework	**Seven-Fold Victory**		
	The Fall of Babylon	17:1–19:10	127
	Beasts Defeated	19:11–21	130
	The Dragon Bound	20:1–10	135
	Judgment	20:11–15	138
	A New Heaven and New Earth	21:1–8	140
	The New Jerusalem	21:9–27	143
	The River of Life	22:1–5	145
5	Review	17:1–22:5	146
Homework	**Revelation as a Whole**		
	Review all previous homework	1:1–22:5	
	Epilogue	22:6–21	157
6	Revelation as a Whole		155

Index

1,260 days, 67, 85
144 thousand, 52, 91
42 months, 66, 88

666, *see* number of the Beast

A little scroll, 63
Alpha and Omega, 1
altar of incense, 55
Among the Lampstands, 11, 14
A New Heaven and New Earth, 140
A New Housecoat, 136
A New Song, 91, 94
apocalypse, *see* revelation
application, 7, 52, 88, 90, 95, 111, 118, 122, 126, 159
A Promised Blessing, xvi
Armageddon, 108
Armor, 97
army, 61, 129
A Roaring Lion, 76
A scroll, 39
Asia, 3, 12
A Thief, 25
A throne, 37
At the Mall, 71
authority, 3, 22–24, 28, 60, 70, 88, 102, 150
A Wedding Invitation, 124
A woman, 80

Babylon, 95, 118, 142, 150
Babylon is fallen, 95
Balaam, 19, 20
battle, 134
    of Armageddon, 108
Beasts, 91

beast from the earth, 89
beast from the sea, 88
four beasts around the throne, 38, 126
the Beast, 89, 96, 108, 119, 130, 137, 150, 151
Beasts Defeated, 130
beatitude
    first, xvi
    second, 93
    third, 25
    fourth, 124
    fifth, 136
    sixth, 114
    seventh, 148
Bible reference
    Genesis
        2:8–9, 16
        3:1–13, 81
        3:17–19,24, 144
        3:22–24, 16
        6:5–8, 103
        10:2, 134
        15:18, 106
        49:9–10, 40
    Exodus
        7:17–25, 106
        9:8–12, 106
        9:13–35, 109
        9:14–16, 106
        9:18–26, 111
        9:27–35, 110
        10:21–23, 106
        16:14–15, 20
        19:4, 85
        19:19, 65

28:15–21, 143
30:1–8, 55, 56
30:6–8, 56
32:32–33, 138
Leviticus
  26:21–26, 45
Numbers
  22:1–25:5, 19, 20
  24:17, 24
Deuteronomy
  8:3, 20
  11:24, 106
  18:4, 92
  32:1–4, 100
  32:24–25, 45
  32:43, 119
Joshua
  12:21, 108
  17:11–12, 108
Judges
  1:27, 108
  4:1–5:31, 110
  5:19, 108, 110
2 Samuel
  6:14–15, 92
1 Kings
  16:29–33, 22
  17:1, 85
  20:13–30, 68
  20:23, 68
2 Kings
  23:29–30, 108
1 Chronicles
  24:1–19, 38
2 Chronicles
  35:20–24, 108
Job
  1:8–10, 81
Psalms
  2:1–3, 107
  2:1–4, 70
  2:7–9, 24
  2:9, 81, 85, 129
  19:7–11, 64
  21:5–7, 115
  33:1–5, 92

40:1–3, 92
69:28, 138
91:5–10, 29
100:4, 70
104:1–35, 34
149:1–4, 92
Proverbs
  3:9–10, 92
Ecclesiastes
  4:1, 88
  11:9, 137
  12:13–14, 137
Song of Songs
  6:10, 81
Isaiah
  6:5, 39
  6:8, 39
  11:1, 41
  14:12, 60
  14:12–15, 83
  21:9, 95
  22:20–22, 29
  35:10, 92
  52:14–53:12, 43
  63:2–4, 99
  64:6, 27
  65:17–19, 140
  66:7, 81
  66:7–13, 81
  66:22–24, 140
Jeremiah
  25:14–29, 97
  7:33, 129
  9:15, 57
  17:7–8, 144
  23:15, 57
  25:10, 123
  51:7–8, 95
  51:45, 122
  51:47–49, 95
  51:49, 119
Lamentations
  3:15, 57
Ezekiel
  2:8–3:3, 65
  3:7, 65

Index

    6:11–14, 45
    9:4, 52
    38:1–39:29, 134
    38:1–5, 134
    40:1–43:12, 66
Daniel
    1:12–14, 18
    2:31–44, 90
    3:1–30, 90
    7:3–12, 88
    10:5–6, 13
    10:13,21, 84
    12:1, 84
    12:4,9–10, 156
Joel
    3:13–14, 99
Amos
    5:7, 57
Zechariah
    1:3, 47
    1:8–10, 45
    4:1–14, 67
    4:6, 67
    6:1–3, 45
    12:10–11, 108
Matthew
    2:2, 80
    6:9–13, 56
    6:19–21, 31
    9:35–38, 98
    10:28, 130
    13:24–30,36–43, 99
    13:38–43, 23
    16:27, 137
    17:1–2, 12
    18:15–17, 23
    18:20, 13
    22:36–40, 14
    23:24–26, 31
    24:14, 95
    24:30, 3
    24:31, 99
    24:42–44, 108
    24:43–44, 26
    24:44, 4
    28:1–6, 135
    28:18–20, 95
Mark
    4:26–29, 98
Luke
    4:16–21, 67
    4:25, 85
    10:17–18, 84
    10:18–19, 60
    12:33–34, 31
    12:35–40, 25
    14:16–24, 124
    21:12–19, 8
John
    1:1–3, 129
    1:9–14, 149
    1:14–17, 129
    1:36, 40
    3:16, xv
    3:36, 112
    4:13–14, 144
    4:14, 105
    4:35–38, 99
    6:35, 20
    7:37–39, 105
    8:12, 143
    10:7–9, 142
    10:27, 89
    10:27–28, 92
    11:24, 137
    12:28–30, 65
    12:48, 130
    13:1–16, 131
    13:35, 15, 21
    14:6, 129
    15:9–17, 21
    16:33, 9
    19:30, 110
Acts
    1:11, 3
    9:22–25, 9
    14:19–20, 9
    27:41–44, 9
Romans
    1:16–17, 95
    1:18, 47
    1:18–19, 74

1:18–20, 95, 112
1:21–23, 105
2:4–6, 72
3:22, 138
3:22–24, 126
4:1–5, 126
6:23, 61, 74, 137
8:22, 35
8:22–23, 74
8:27, 55
8:33–34, 83
8:35–37, 9
8:38–39, 9
12:1–2, 133
13:11–14, 27
14:17, 105
16:17–18, 22
1 Corinthians
  1:11–13, 143
  3:3–9, 143
  3:11–13, 31
  3:16, 66
  5:9–11, 123
  13:2, 6, 160
  14:8, 72
  15:22–25, 135
  15:26–27, 138
  15:51–52, 65
  15:51–57, 3, 134
  15:54–57, 138
2 Corinthians
  6:14–7:1, 123
  10:3–5, 96
  11:3, 83
Galatians
  5:19–21, 61
  5:22–23, 144, 145
Ephesians
  1:13–14, 52, 153
  2:8–10, 127
  5:5, 90
  5:5–6, 112
  5:25–32, 126
  6:10–13, 77
  6:10–20, 97
  6:12, 90
  6:17, 13, 78
Philippians
  1:19–21, 93
  4:3, 138
Colossians
  1:16, 1
  2:8, 134
1 Thessalonians
  4:13–18, 67
  4:16, 65
  4:16–18, 3
2 Timothy
  3:1–5, 122
  3:16–17, 2
Hebrews
  4:12, 13
  4:16, 55
  8:1–2, 55
  9:27, 3
  11:9–10, 142
  11:10, 144
  11:37–39, 45
  12:2, 17
  13:8, 1
James
  1:18, 92
  2:17–18, 127
  5:16–18, 67
  5:17, 85
1 Peter
  2:5, 66
  2:9, 3
  4:12–16, 17
  5:6–11, 76
  5:8–9, 60
2 Peter
  1:19–21, xvi
  2:14–16, 19
  3:3–10, 71
  3:3–13, 4
  3:8–9, 47
  3:9, 7, 52, 72
  3:10–13, 140
Jude
  1:6, 108
  1:9, 84

Index

Revelation
- 1:1, 149
- 1:1–8, 4, 152
- 1:3, xv, xvi, 1, 4
- 1:5, 129, 153, 154
- 1:8, 13, 140
- 1:9, 12
- 1:9–20, 14, 152
- 1:9–3:22, 33
- 1:14, 129
- 1:15, 65
- 1:16, 13, 65, 129
- 1:20, 67
- 2:1–7, 16
- 2:5, 152
- 2:6, 16
- 2:7, 9
- 2:8–11, 18
- 2:10, 153
- 2:10,13, 134
- 2:11, 9, 134
- 2:12, 129
- 2:12–17, 20
- 2:13, 153
- 2:15, 16
- 2:16, 152
- 2:17, 9
- 2:18–29, 24
- 2:19, 153
- 2:25, 24
- 2:26–28, 9
- 2:27, 81, 129, 154
- 3:1–6, 27
- 3:3, 152
- 3:5, 9, 138
- 3:7–13, 30
- 3:12, 9
- 3:14, 129, 153
- 3:14–22, 31
- 3:19, 152
- 3:21, 9
- 4:1–11, 152
- 4:1–11:19, 75
- 4:1–5:14, 41
- 4:3, 65
- 4:4, 126
- 4:6, 102, 126
- 4:11, 34
- 5:1–14, 152
- 5:5, 65
- 5:9–10, 40
- 5:12, 40
- 5:13, 40
- 6:1–17, 49
- 6:6, 45
- 6:9, 8
- 6:9–11, 154
- 6:10, 154
- 6:15–17, 47, 73
- 7:1–17, 53
- 7:3–8, 91, 153
- 7:9, 126
- 7:9–17, 152
- 7:14, 52
- 8:1–5, 56
- 8:6–9:21, 61
- 8:8–9, 106
- 8:10–11, 106
- 8:13, 55
- 9:4, 91, 153
- 9:12, 55
- 9:13–19, 106
- 9:20–21, 61, 63, 71, 72, 152
- 10:1–11:13, 69
- 10:6, 65
- 10:10–11, 64, 153
- 10:11, 69
- 11:3, 153
- 11:7–10, 154
- 11:10, 154
- 11:14, 55
- 11:14–19, 72
- 11:15, 154
- 11:15–19, 152
- 11:17, 68
- 11:18, 154
- 11:19, 110
- 12:1, 78
- 12:1–16:21, 113
- 12:1–17, 85
- 12:5, 81, 129, 154
- 12:9, 76

12:10, 84
12:10–12, 152
12:11, 32
12:17, 87
12:18, 87
12:18–13:18, 91
13:1, 87, 105, 119
13:1,11, 130
13:8, 88
13:9, 88
13:15, 134, 154
13:16, 130
13:16–17, 91, 104, 134
14:1–5, 94, 153
14:6–13, 97
14:6–7, 153
14:7, 154
14:8, 110, 118, 119
14:9–10, 102
14:9–12, 104
14:12, 102
14:13, 93
14:14–20, 99
14:19–20, 129
15:1–8, 103
15:3–4, 152
15:4, 100, 105
16:1–12, 107
16:7, 154
16:9,11, 153
16:13, 130
16:13–16, 108
16:14,16, 130
16:15, 25
16:17–21, 111
16:19, 118
16:21, 109
17:1, 154
17:1–19:10, 127
17:1–22:5, 146
17:2, 123
17:6, 119, 154
17:8–12, 119
17:9, 83, 119
17:12, 83
17:13–14, 130

17:14, 129, 153
17:15, 123
17:18, 118
18:3, 119, 123
18:8, 154
18:10, 154
18:20, 119, 154
18:24, 154
19:1–8, 152
19:2, 119, 154
19:5, 85
19:5-10, 92
19:6, 154
19:8, 31, 126, 127, 129, 131
19:9, 124, 127
19:11, 153, 154
19:11–21, 130
19:15, 129, 154
19:20, 89
20:1–10, 135
20:4, 154
20:4, 6, 154
20:6, 136
20:11–15, 138
20:12–13, 154
20:14, 18
21:1–8, 140
21:2, 142
21:5, 153
21:9–27, 143
22:1–5, 145
22:4, 153
22:6, 153
22:6–21, 157
22:7, 114
22:14, 148
22:20, 157
Big Brother, 87
birth, 81
Bitter-Sweet, 64
blood of Jesus, 84
Book
    of Life, 138
book
    of life, 88, 150
    sweet and bitter, 65

Index

with seven seals, 40, 72, 150
bowl, *see* Plagues
bride of the Lamb, 126, 150
bugle, *see* trumpet
Bugle Calls, 53

catacombs, 16
Catastrophes, 56
cavalry, 61
chronology, 7
church, 21, 150
    first, *see* Ephesus
    second, *see* Smyrna
    third, *see* Pergamum
    fourth, *see* Thyatira
    fifth, *see* Sardis
    sixth, *see* Philadelphia
    seventh, *see* Laodicea
city of God, 144
Come, Lord Jesus, 155
Conclusion, 149
conquer, 45
constellations, 80
Creation Groans, 35
crown
    of life, 18
    rainbow, 63
    ten crowns of the Beast, 88

Dürer, Albrecht, 43
Daniel, 18
darkness, 57, 105
day
    of the Lord, 140
    The Great Day, 108
death, 45
    first, 137
    second, 18, 137, 150
    the last enemy, 138
dedication, 84
diabolos (*Strong's* No. 1228), 81
discipline, 23
discussion, 159
Down by the Riverside, 144
Dragon, 81, 108
drunkenness, 96

eagle, 85
earth
    new, 140
earthquake, 67, 70, 110
economics, 90
elders, 38, 70, 126
Elijah, 67, 85
Ephesus, 15, 16, 29, 150
Epilogue, 157
eternal, 3
Euphrates River, 106
eye salve, 31
eyes of Jesus, 13, 22, 129

face like the sun, 65
Faithful, 153
faithful, 29
Fallen, 120
Fall of Babylon, 95, 110, 123, 151
false doctrine, 19
False Prophet, 89, 96, 108, 130, 137, 150, 151
feet
    of fire, 65
    of Jesus, 13, 22
Finished, 110
fire, 61
first fruits, 92
flood, 85
followers of the Lamb, 92
forehead, 52
For Group Study, 159
For Who He Is, 100
foundation
    twelve foundations, 142
Four seals, 45
Four trumpets, 57
fruit, 144

Garden of Eden, 16
garments
    white, 27, 31, 126, 150
gate
    twelve gates, 142
Gathering for War, 107
Gog, 134

gold, 31
gospel, 95, 151
Grapes, 99
group study, 159

hailstorm, 70, 110
Hallelujah, 123
hand of Jesus, 13, 26
Harvests, 98
    of grain, 98
    of grapes, 99
head
    seven heads of dragon, 83
    seven heads of the Beast, 119
heaven
    new, 140
Holy, Holy, Holy, 37
Holy of Holies, 102
Holy Spirit, 52, 60
horn
    ten horns of dragon, 83
    ten horns of the Beast, 88, 119, 130
horseman
    four horsemen, 45
    on white horse, 129
Horsemen and More, 43

idolatry, 20, 22, 89, 123
immorality, 20
In-Depth Plan, 161
Incense, 55, 56
interlude, 52, 63, 98, 108, 151
interpretation, 6, 11, 47, 52, 72, 81, 88, 108, 118, 123, 156, 159
Interpreting the seals, 47
Interpreting the trumpets, 61
Introduction, 1

Jerusalem, 142
    new, 150
Jesus reigns, 154
Jesus wins, 152
Jezebel, 22, 24
Jonestown, 21
Judgment, 138, 154

key of David, 28
King of Kings, 69, 129

lamb
    False Prophet, 89
    of God, 40, 43, 92, 126
lampstands, 13, 67
Laodicea, 31, 150
leader, 22, 24
letter, 2, 12
liar
    not, no guile, 92
lightning, 70, 110
linen of the bride, 126, 150
lion of Judah, 40
locusts, 60
logos (*Strong's* No. 3056), 13
Lord of Lords, 129
love, 21
    brotherly love, 21
    first love, 15
lukewarm, 31

machaira (*Strong's* No. 3162), 13
Magog, 134
manna, 20, 150
mark
    of God's seal, 52, 60, 91
    of the Beast, 90, 96, 104, 130, 151
Mark of the Beast, 96
marriage, 16
Martyrs, 153
martyrs, 45, 67, 119
materialism, 90
Measurements, 65
Megiddo, 108
messenger, 13
Michael, 84
millennium, 134, 150
Moses, 67
mourn, 3
multitude, 52
My Witnesses, 63, 69

Nicolaitans, 15, 19

Index

No-Homework Plan, 160
number of the Beast, 90

open door, 30
outline, 5, 9, 35, 53, 78, 101, 115, 149
Overcomers, 7, 9, 84
Overview Plan, 163

Panorama, 4, 72, 149, 154
patience, 22
Pergamum, 19, 20, 24, 150
persecution, 18
Philadelphia, 29, 30, 150
pillar, 30, 150
Plagues, 45, 78, 103, 111
    first, 104
    second, 105
    third, 105
    fourth, 105
    fifth, 105
    sixth, 106
    seventh, 110
power, 88
prayer, 55
Prologue, 4

Quick Overview Plan, 165

rainbow, 63
Reapings, 99
repent, 7, 15, 20, 23, 26, 31, 32, 41, 47, 49, 52, 53, 61, 72, 74, 105, 110
Repentance, 152
Reservations Suggested, 148
resurrection
    for judgment, 3, 137
    of believers, 3, 134
    of Jesus, 3, 13, 17
revelation
    apokalupsis, 2
Revelation as a Whole, 155
Reverend Jezebel's Church, 21
Review, 32, 72, 111, 145
Review—A Scroll with Seven Seals, 75

Review—Letters to Seven Churches, 33
Review—Seven-Fold Victory, 146
Review—Seven Signs, 113
rhema (*Strong's* No. 4487), 13
rhomphaia (*Strong's* No. 4501), 13
righteousness, 27
    dikaiomata, 126
    of the saints, 126
River of Life, 144
robe dipped in blood, 129
rocks, 49
rod of iron, 24, 81, 129
Root of David, 41

sackcloth, 67
Sardis, 26, 27, 150
sash of Jesus, 13, 28
Satan, 18, 20, 81, 133, 138, 151
Satan (*Strong's* No. 4567), 81
Satan (*Strong's* No. 7854), 81
Satan bound, 133
scales, 45
scepter, *see* rod of iron
scroll, *see* book
sea
    became blood, 57, 105
    of glass, 38, 102
seal
    first, 45
    second, 45
    third, 45
    fourth, 45
    fifth, 45
    sixth, 47
    seventh, 55
    of God, *see* mark of God's seal
Sealed, 153
second coming, 3, 25, 27
serpent, 133
Servants of God, 53
shepherd, 53
sign, 78, 111, 151
    first, *see* woman clothed with the sun
    second, *see* beast from the sea

third, *see* A New Song
fourth, *see* gospel
fifth, *see* Fall of Babylon
sixth, *see* mark of the Beast
seventh, *see* Plagues
signet, 39, 52
silence, 55
Six Bowls, 107
Six Seals, 49
Six Trumpets, 61
Smyrna, 17, 18, 29, 150
Songs, 92, 103, 151
son of man, 98
star
    Lucifer, 60
    morning, 24
    seven stars, 13
    stars swept from heaven, 83
stone
    twelve precious stones, 143
sun
    blackened, *see* darkness
    scorching, 105
sword, 13, 19, 21, 45, 129
    machaira, 13
    rhomphaia, 13
symbols, 11, 14, 123

tactic, 89, 90, 92, 96
tapestry, 7
tares, 23
temple, 102, 150
    measure, 66
ten days, 18
testimony, 84, 85
The Almighty, 68
The Beast, 87
The Choir, 101
The Church, 21
The church must overcome, 150
The City of God, 141
The Creator, 34
The Defeat of Oppression, 128
The devil is angry, 151
The Downtown Church, 14
The Dragon, 85
The Dragon Bound, 135
The End of Deception, 131
The Faithful, 49
The Fall of Babylon, 127
The Fall of Civilization, 117
The False Prophet, 89
The fifth seal, 45
The final deception, 134
The gospel, 95
The Hail Storm, 109
The Historic Church, 26
The Lamb, 43
The Last Enemy, 135
The Liberation of Creation, 139
The millennium, 134
The New Jerusalem, 143
The Obscure Church, 28
The Permissive Church, 19
The prostitute, 117
The Real Superhero, 114
The River of Life, 145
The Seventh Bowl, 111
The Seventh Trumpet, 72
The sixth seal, 47
The Suburban Church, 30
The Testimony of Martyrs , 8
The Throne of God, 41
The Underground Church, 16
The world must repent, 150
The Wrath of God, 101
thief, 25, 26
thlipsis (*Strong's* No. 2346), 12
thousand years, *see* millennium
Three Angels, 97
Three Frogs, 108
Three Weapons, 94
throne
    great white, 137
    of saints, 150
Throne of God, 38, 102, 144
thunder, 70, 110
Thyatira, 22, 24, 150
translation, 4
treasure in heaven, 31
tree
    burned, 57

Index

    of life, 16, 144, 150
    two olive trees, 67
tribulation
    thlipsis, 12
    great, 52
trumpet, 72
    first, 57
    second, 57
    third, 57
    fourth, 57
    fifth, 60
    sixth, 61
    seventh, 70, 110
    last, 65
    seven trumpets, 55, 151

undefiled, 92
underground church, 16

Victory, 7, 115, 152
    first, 118, 127, 150
    second, 128, 130, 150
    third, 133, 135
    fourth, 137, 138, 150
    fifth, 140, 150
    sixth, 142, 143, 150
    seventh, 144, 145, 150
virgins, 92
voice
    like lion, 65
    of Jesus, 13
    thunder, 65

War, 77
Warfare, 7, 84, 85, 90, 92, 96, 101, 111
War in Heaven, 80
War in heaven, 83
War on Earth, 84
Washing Feet, 131
water
    became blood, 105
    many waters of the prostitute, 123
    of life, 156
    poisoned, 57

weapon, 92, 95, 96, 101, 151
wedding, 31, 126
Wheat, 98
wilderness, 81
wind, 52
wine press, 99, 129
witness
    faithful, 129
Witnesses
    two, 67
woe, 55, 59
    first, 60
    second, 61
    third, 70
Woes, 59
woman
    clothed with the sun, 81, 85
    prostitute, 118
word
    logos, 13, 129
    rhema, 13
Work that Lasts, 93
wormwood, 57
Worship, 152
worship, 53, 156

zōon (*Strong's* No. 2198), 38

About the author

Edward B. Allen is the author of books for three styles of devotional Bible study. Verse-by-verse books draw devotional points from the Scripture passage in sequence. Historical-people books focus on incidents in the lives of historical people that illustrate biblical principles. Topical books explore relevant Scriptures throughout the Bible. His books also include many personal stories from modern life.

His books are in two series. Books in the *A Slow Walk* series have short meditations in daily-devotional format, such as *A Slow Walk through Psalm 119: 90 Devotional Meditations*. Books in the *Devotional Commentary* series are straight reads with a devotional slant, rather than academic or theological comments, such as *Practical Faith: A Devotional Commentary*.

He has led discussion Bible-study groups in evangelical churches for over 50 years He received a Ph.D. in Computer Science degree at Florida Atlantic University and had a career in software engineering. He has authored or coauthored over 80 professional papers.